# THE PSYCHOLOGY OF DEMOCRACY

What is a democracy? Why do we form democratic systems? Can democracy survive in an age of distrust and polarisation?

The Psychology of Democracy explains the psychological underpinnings behind why people engage with and participate in politics. Covering the influence that political campaigns and media play, the book analyses topical and real-world political events including the Arab Spring, Brexit, Black Lives Matter, the US 2020 elections and the Covid-19 pandemic. Lilleker and Ozgul take the reader on a journey to explore the cognitive processes at play when engaging with a political news item all the way through to taking to the streets to protest government policy and action.

In an age of post-truth and populism, The Psychology of Democracy shows us how a strong and healthy democracy depends upon the feelings and emotions of its citizens, including trust, belonging, empowerment and representation, as much as on electoral processes.

**Darren G. Lilleker** is Associate Professor in Political Communication at Bournemouth University, UK, and author of Political Communication and Cognition (Palgrave, 2014).

**Billur Aslan Ozgul** is Lecturer in Political Communication at Brunel University London, UK, and author of the book Leading Protests in the Digital Age: Youth Activism in Egypt and Syria (Palgrave, 2020).

# THE PSYCHOLOGY OF EVERYTHING

People are fascinated by psychology, and what makes humans tick. Why do we think and behave the way we do? We've all met armchair psychologists claiming to have the answers, and people that ask if psychologists can tell what they're thinking. The Psychology of Everything is a series of books which debunk the popular myths and pseudo-science surrounding some of life's biggest questions.

The series explores the hidden psychological factors that drive us, from our subconscious desires and aversions, to our natural social instincts. Absorbing, informative, and always intriguing, each book is written by an expert in the field, examining how research-based knowledge compares with popular wisdom, and showing how psychology can truly enrich our understanding of modern life.

Applying a psychological lens to an array of topics and contemporary concerns – from sex, to fashion, to conspiracy theories – The Psychology of Everything will make you look at everything in a new way.

Titles in the series:

For further information about this series please visit www.routledgetextbooks.com/textbooks/thepsychologyofeverything/

# THE PSYCHOLOGY OF DEMOCRACY

DARREN G. LILLEKER AND BILLUR ASLAN OZGUL

Routledge
Taylor & Francis Group

LONDON AND NEW YORK

First published 2022
by Routledge
2 Park Square, Milton Park, Abingdon, Oxon OX14 4RN

and by Routledge
605 Third Avenue, New York, NY 10158

Routledge is an imprint of the Taylor & Francis Group, an informa business

British Library Cataloguing-in-Publication Data
A catalogue record for this book is available from the British Library

Library of Congress Cataloging-in-Publication Data
A catalog record for this book has been requested

ISBN: 978-0-367-89816-8 (hbk)
ISBN: 978-0-367-89817-5 (pbk)
ISBN: 978-1-003-02129-2 (ebk)

DOI: 10.4324/9781003021292

Typeset in Joanna
by Apex CoVantage, LLC

# CONTENTS

# INTRODUCTION: UNDERSTANDING DEMOCRACY

The simplest way to understand democracy is to look at the origins of the word, and its definition as 'people power'. The citizens of a democratic nation possess a degree of control over both the values that imbue the governance of their nations and the policies implemented. In practice, this means that through a variety of forms of participation in political activities, from the formal processes of voting to acts of petitioning or protest. Citizens can collectively influence the composition of the legislature and the policies that are enacted. However, voting is often privileged in discussions of political participation. This is because most democratic nations operate with a representative system. Citizens vote in elections to elect the representatives who sit in parliament, a group of whom will form a government and enact the policies they proposed in their election campaign manifestos. Political parties provide the structure for representative democracy as they allow representatives to unite around a set of ideas which, theoretically at least, offer voters clear choices.

Research has, perhaps somewhat simplistically, suggested that citizens learn to see the world through an ideological framework (socialism, liberalism, conservatism) which imposes constraints on issues. One can only see an issue within set boundaries, so support for party issue positions is determined by each individual's ideological frame of reference. Depending on where someone is positioned on the ideological spectrum, any given political approach may be more or less acceptable. Hence the traditional view of voting is that citizens will make their selection based on the extent that a party position on an issue of importance aligns with their own. However, research has also shown that a range of factors influence voter choices while party attachment or alignment with a particular ideology have been in significant decline over the last four or five decades (Dalton, 2013). The various factors, which include assessments of the relevance of party promises, the prominence and characteristics of leaders as well as a broad range of mental associations which are learned about parties and individuals, will be explored in more detail throughout this book. However, at this stage it is important to emphasise that voting is not only based on the ideological position of a candidate or party. Evidence suggests there is a combination of value driven factors alongside those that follow more economic calculations, where voters assess whether the policies of one individual candidate or party will have a positive outcome for them as an individual, their community or perhaps the nation as a whole. The former factors suggest that image and the party brand are important, the latter suggests a greater focus on policy. Either way, at the heart of democracy is the idea that citizens have a clear choice presented to them and the election campaign should encourage citizens to desire the election of one party or candidate in comparison to their rivals. The strength of positive feelings towards the chosen party or candidate, as well as the strength of negative feelings towards the alternatives, should determine the extent to which the outcome of democratic procedures, such as elections, produce satisfied citizens.

Yet many citizens of democracies exhibit the signs of being highly dissatisfied. When an election produces a clear victory for a party, one might argue that the majority should accept the outcome of the contest, the legitimacy of the result and the consequent government and be able to trust that government to fulfil its promises while also ensuring that the interests of the entire country are protected. However, there are minimal rules to ensure a party elected must honour all or even any of its manifesto pledges. Obviously, they risk negative ratings and being ousted at the next election, but with a clear majority in the legislature, a government can do as it wishes. Outside of a small number of democracies, it is rare for one party to win a clear majority and a coalition must be formed. Parties which join forces to form a government necessarily have to arrive at negotiated compromises. The forced abandonment of manifesto pledges can mean that the coalition pleases only a section of those who voted for the parties that form the government. Independent of whether pledges are kept or not, the promised societal benefits of pledges may not be felt by voters. A government may have been elected to put in place certain policies to improve overall standards of living. If those policies are enacted but standards of living do not improve or are not perceived to improve to the extent voters expected, then, as with breaking pledges, voters may feel betrayed. Furthermore, voters with strong negative feelings towards those elected may never fully accept the legitimacy of that government, particularly if it acts in ways that they feel counter the overall values of their nation. Thus, the judgments citizens make about the performance of political institutions may often be based on perceptions and feelings. Citizens may evaluate their relationship with democratic structures as part of the 'demos' (people) and the extent that their democratic system makes them feel they possess 'kratos' (power). While all citizens may legally have equality in terms of the ability to vote, they may not feel they have equal levels of influence. Hence, how citizens feel, what we call here the psychology of democracy, is of significant importance if we are to assess the health of any given democracy and its processes.

## THE HEALTH OF DEMOCRACY

The previous section suggests a certain fragility which can undermine our democracies. We would not play down this fragility. For a democracy to be truly strong and healthy the citizens of a democratic nation should trust in the institutions of democracy, not necessarily trusting all politicians, as scepticism is healthy, but that the system of democracy will protect citizens against self-seeking, dishonest or corrupt actors. Citizens should also feel they have some degree of power and influence, and that at minimum, when they express their views, law makers will listen and honestly respond to their concerns. These are basic conditions which constitute positive feelings of empowerment and belonging that the majority of citizens should experience.

We can, however, measure the quality of a democracy and it is important to understand that not all nations that claim to be democracies score 100% on such measures. One widely referenced measurement schematic is The Democracy Index produced by the Economist Intelligence Unit (EIU). The EIU index measures five core dimensions which constitute the basis for a well-functioning democracy. The first dimension focuses on the electoral processes, in particular whether anyone can stand for election and the extent that all citizens, with some accepted restrictions due to age, are able to participate within the electorate as well as whether any party can in theory be elected and power can transfer smoothly. The second dimension explores the functioning of government. Here there are measures on the checks and balances which moderate government authority, levels of accountability and corruption as well as public confidence in these institutions. The latter perhaps being crucial as it measures the gap, if it exists, between how a system works theoretically and how citizens feel and experience the workings of democratic institutions. This book will show that the confidence of citizens in the institutions might increase or decrease based on emotional factors. Hence, even the quality of a democracy in a country depends on the feelings of its citizens, how they perceive the democracy in that country. The third dimension reinforces the focus on the psychological aspects of a democracy by focusing on political participation. The measures here focus on voter turnout, equality of representation across the genders and minority groups as well as engagement and knowledge about the nation's politics. The fourth dimension is the democratic political culture and measures the perceptions citizens hold of the current government and alternatives, including support for military or authoritarian rule to replace democratic institutions.

This dimension thus focuses on the extent to which popular support for democracy is embedded. The fifth and final dimension focuses on the upholding and protection of civil liberties in a country. Basically, this measures whether citizens are free to think and act politically and socially. Measures include whether the media is free of government control, whether access to the Internet is unfettered, whether the judiciary branch is independent and whether citizens are treated equally within legal processes.

The Economic Intelligence Unit (2019) Index shows that 22 nations (13.2%) are full democracies; 54 (32.3%) are flawed democracies; 37 (22.2%) are hybrid regimes, where elections are held but are not free and fair, corruption is widespread and civil society, and its associated freedoms, are weak; and 54 (32.3%) are authoritarian regimes. The world's population who live in full democracies is only 5.7%, over a third (35.6%) live under authoritarian rule and nearly half (42.7%) live in flawed democracies. The nature of the regime thus shapes the psychology within that nation. The index also demonstrates that democracy is retreating globally, and not just in parts of the world known for corrupt and unstable governance. EIU analysts attribute the decline of democracy to increased emphasis on managerialist governance; the growing influence of unelected and unaccountable institutions; the extent that substantive issues of national importance are determined by politicians, experts or supranational bodies without any accountability to the citizens; a perceived widening gap between political elites and citizens; and a curtailment of fundamental freedoms such as of media and speech. The result is an average, although reasonably small, negative difference in democracy level between 2009–2018 on all dimensions except political participation. This suggests that a more people are engaged in politics, and if they are angry at the anti-democratic drift, they are willing to ensure their voices are heard. Hence, we suggest that democracy may be stuttering, for a number of reasons associated with global capitalism, the devolution of power to supranational entities and the composition of individual governments; however, while more democracies may have significant flaws there is also a vibrancy and a public drive to reclaim their 'kratos'.

So which countries' citizens enjoy the most complete forms of democracy? There is a small group of countries who score over nine on the Index's ten-point scale. In order, they are Norway, Iceland, Sweden, New Zealand, Finland, Ireland, Denmark, Canada, Australia, Switzerland and the Netherlands. Scoring between eight and nine, from highest to lowest, are Luxembourg, Germany, the UK, Uruguay, Austria, Spain, Mauritius, Costa Rica, France, Chile and Portugal. The make up the group of fully democratic nations. In 2019, the United States dropped into the flawed democracy category, scoring 7.96 out of ten, it sits alongside South Korea, Japan and Italy, many of the CEE countries that have only experienced 30 years of democracy following the collapse of the Soviet control and many African nations which have struggled to find stability and overcome their history as part of a European empire. Some of these nations, as well as many in South America and Asia, are hybrid regimes. Many also live under authoritarian rule. Yet even under the yoke of authoritarianism we find scores of 5–6 for political culture in some countries who are overall full democracies, and where the human demand for freedom is not absent but is simply suppressed. The culture required for democratic engagement exists and perhaps conditions are ripe in many parts of the world for greater sovereignty to be awarded its people.

Within this work we draw our examples from full or flawed democracies, after all, our aim is to examine how people think and act within nations where they are free to do so. However, this book reveals that independent of whether someone is born Norwegian or Chilean, Palestinian or Zimbabwean we are composed of the same human impulses and drives. The conditions experienced by a Zimbabwean would be entirely alien to a Norwegian, yet how they navigate their worlds are driven by the same cognitive processes. So, one of our aims is to explain these general cognitive processes. On the other hand, the Zimbabwean and Norwegian people differ due to their experiences and how they have been led to understand how the world operates. Hence, we also show that 1) citizens' identities and social norms 2) the actions and communications of political organisations 3) the mediation of politics and 4) past experiences and the actions of other citizens, all play a significant role in shaping cognitive processes and emotional states within democratic nations. We discuss how these four factors shape citizens' feelings and consequently influence their political thinking, protest activities and voting in each chapter.

## STRUCTURE OF THE BOOK

Within the first chapter we focus on some of the core tenets of democracy, the nature of empowerment, how identities are created and how these link to values which form a cognitive framework for understand ourselves, our communities and the world around us. The experiences of those in full democracies, like our Norwegian, will be very different from those who scrape together an existence in the unequal and oppressive authoritarian regimes towards the bottom of the index as our Zimbabwean does.

Socialisation processes, the subject of Chapter 2, reinforces the importance of lived environments and experiences for understanding how people think about democracy, its processes and institutions. Within this chapter we explore the power of dominant narratives and the importance for democracy of open and pluralist debate and the emergence of counternarratives. While we expect citizens of full democracies to have access to a range of counternarratives, the fact that one narrative dominates and defines citizens' places in society, their access to influence, and their access to the benefits of a society are likely factors that shape the differential scores for political culture the EIU analysts find in their data. We also here highlight the challenges posed for democracy from lazy thinking and a reliance on simplistic forms of communication. Particular problems arise when citizens process political communication through the lens of pre-existing prejudices and bias and how, in a digital age, this can contribute to societal polarisation.

This leads on to a discussion of manipulation. In Chapter 3, using the complementary lenses of proximity and valence we explore how citizens think about politics, what it is that they seek and how political campaigns attempt to make one program more cognitively accessible and resonant than alternatives. Here it is important to remember the separation between campaigning and governance. Campaigning is designed to sell a program in order to win power. Governance on the other hand is about implementation and management of the nation. There is a natural separation between the two acts because campaigns tap into the hopes and desires of citizens, governance however must deal with the reality of navigating the nation through events which may be out of national control. It is important therefore to consider what sovereignty any nation can enjoy in an interdependent global system and therefore the impact on the citizen who places their hopes in the person they feel closest to, who talks about the issues that concern them most, but then fails to deliver once elected.

In the Chapter 4, we focus on participation. A nation cannot truly be a democracy unless there is a strong civil society. At points we may feel that our Zimbabwean is more likely to take part in protests than the average Norwegian. Is that because the Zimbabwean faces a daily threat to their survival and so their only recourse is to take to the streets? Basically, is the Norwegian living such a comfortable life that they feel no need to break from their routines to engage in political activism? Alternatively, is participation driven by self-efficacy and does the Zimbabwean feel they can have an impact whereas the Norwegian feels apathetic about the possibility of political change? These questions are discussed within the context of the range or forms of participation that can be enjoyed within advanced democracies. Alongside considering voting and protesting, we consider what role simple actions such as petitioning, or liking and sharing content on social media platforms, play in sustaining an active civil society.

Our concluding chapter (chapter 5) retraces the central arguments of the book. We also discuss the human impulses and drivers that have shaped nation-specific attitudes towards democracy during the Covid-19 pandemic. Cumulatively, we want to get the reader thinking about how democracies work. Not about how the institutions operate but to think about the relationship between the represented and the representative, the citizen and the governor. In democracies, there should be no such thing as an elite and a mass, rather both are part of the citizenry and at least in theory any citizen can rise to be part of the governing group. Equally, all citizens are equal in enjoying rights, freedoms, influence and the holding of those who govern to account. But, practically, are these mechanisms working? Do citizens feel they are part of a citizenry, enjoying the full freedoms and benefits of a society, or do some feel excluded and marginalised? These factors all constitute the psychology of democracy and how we as people think about the political processes which shape our existence. Hence, they are of fundamental importance for understanding the workings of our democracies, whether they are full or flawed, and why some people's experiences differ from the outcomes of scores against measures such as that developed by the EIU.

## BIBLIOGRAPHY

Dalton, R. J. (2013). Citizen politics: Public opinion and political parties in advanced industrial democracies. CQ Press.

Economist Intelligence Unit (2019). Democracy Index 2019: A year of democratic setbacks and popular protest. www.eiu.com

# 1

---

## THE EMOTIONAL CITIZEN

### TRUST IN DEMOCRACIES

It is thus germane to consider that there are many other reasons, beyond parties breaking their pledges, for citizens to question the workings of their nation's democracy. Underpinning most of these reasons is trust: trust in the institutions of democracy to work in the best interests of the people. The point however is not how trust in democracy is broken but how certain mechanisms underpin the maintenance of trust. We argue that democracy is predicated on feelings and emotions: feelings of belonging (a shared identity), empowerment (feeling one has influence over the values and policies of government) and of representation (feeling that one can speak out and be listened to). The extent that citizens feel represented, empowered and that they belong shapes their own trust in and engagement with democratic processes as well as the general public mood. In an age described as one of anger, post-factual democracy and populism, understanding the emotions and feelings that exist and how they are formed is of crucial importance.

The feelings one might possess are engendered through interactions with individuals and organisations which constitute what we refer to as the political sphere: governments, ministries, departments of local and national governance, parties, elected and would-be elected individuals, activists, pressure and protest groups. All these, but particularly organisations that offer representation, are an important part of democratic culture and through their actions (their embodiment of democratic principles) and their communication (their interpretation of democratic life) they impact political culture and shape the public mood. Thus, in beginning our discussion of the psychology of democracy, we introduce how the felt emotional responses to interactions with political institutions influence the public mood and engender trust. Deconstructing this, we introduce notions of empowerment and how the values an individual possesses aid an interpretation of representative actors and organisations and the extent that interactions with the world we navigate chime or contrast with personal values. We argue that the dynamic nature of interactions and emotions provides a baseline for understanding the relationship citizens may have to their polities.

## EMPOWERMENT

To be empowered suggests not just having the theoretical ability to exert influence, as being able to vote might suggest, but that citizens feel their actions can be influential. Hence there is a question as to whether the democratic mechanisms which award power to the citizens are perceived as matching actual citizens' ideals and expectations. Some may vote out of a sense of duty, recognising that one single vote can have limited impact on the outcome of an election or referendum. However, a vote cast for a party which reneges on its promises can be highly disempowering, more so than having one's preferred party lose the election. Similarly, if one stands alongside large numbers to protest against government action and is ignored, one can feel disempowered. The attitude towards participation and the impact activism should have depends on how we are socialised to understand our role as a citizen of a democratic society.

The extent that democratic education is part of the curriculum is sporadic. Rather, most citizens who are born and socialised within democracies learn through everyday contact with individuals and institutions. Parental views on voting, governmental performance, the values of parties and the general efficacy of the system can be highly influential. Schooling may also offer a range of insights, through learning about history, religion and society, young people's world views can develop. When talking of world views, we mean how an individual judges their community, nation and the wider environment as well as their relationship to those elements. World views are often normative claims of how the world should be. The more homogenous, or less diverse, the perspectives an individual receives at home and school, the more set their world view might be when they arrive at voting age. Physical and social mobility can also be significant in supporting the development of a world view; low mobility leads world views to harden, high mobility broadens perspectives. Spending time in other areas of a nation, or other nations, widens knowledge and understanding to an extent. Similarly, university education encourages young people to develop critical thinking skills, enabling them to reflect on their own world views, learn the world views of others and develop a more profound understanding of the world they inhabit.

A key aspect of world views is the extent to which an individual expects to experience empowerment. Intersectionality shows how societies are internally divided by their perceived proximity to power. Structural inequities affect citizens differentially depending on their ethnic backgrounds, religions and social classes, and intersecting those are gender and sexuality factors. Evidence suggests that minority communities feel disempowerment most, and within those communities, females are more politically disempowered than males. Hence viewing communities intersectionally is useful as a baseline for understanding the extent that a community will feel they belong, are represented and have influence (on intersectionality see Hancock, 2016). Differences along these lines may also determine the prevailing world view individuals are most likely to hold. Perhaps logically, those with the most insular world views are also those that are the most deprived and disempowered. These communities share the lowest levels of self-efficacy: the feeling of having power and influence. These communities usually stand in stark contrast to the more affluent regions, where there are higher levels of self-efficacy due to a high preponderance of residents who represent the middle and upper middle classes who tend to also have economic and political influence. While this simplifies the scaled variances across a society for feelings of empowerment, it is often recognised that societies consist of groups which can be separated to some extent into 'haves' and 'have-nots'. The have-nots may be highly diverse, at least in terms of their ethnic and religious make-up, however, among the things that unite the have-nots is a lack of self-efficacy. The world views possessed by members of insular, have-not communities tend to be less diverse, at least in terms of social class, and they are likely to have a narrow world view which perpetuates through generations and peer groups. Members of these communities are least likely to enjoy physical or social mobility, have a basic level of education and are least likely to enjoy informal or social contact with those of other social classes. Unsurprisingly, within such communities, there is a higher propensity to mistrust elites, feel that democracy is not working for them, and feel that they lack meaningful representation. Opinion poll data covering social and political attitudes show that those within social class D (semi-skilled or unskilled workers) are most likely to feel marginalised, and that greater efficacy is felt higher up the social scale. Those from the more deprived communities are only likely to feel less marginalized if they achieve in education, go to university and so enjoy higher levels of social mobility. The size of the broad have-not community may well be a key measure of how well a democracy is performing. The scale of inequality and size of a have-not community is not only a measure of democracy. Serious inequality, as we will discuss later, leads have-nots to support populist political projects which they see as offering a more authentic form of representation. Hence have-nots may pursue anti-democratic means to overcome inequality due to the perceived lack of efficacy offered by traditional means of democratic participation.

## IDENTITIES AND SOCIAL NORMS

Have-nots within a society may not be entirely disengaged from all aspects of politics. The marginalisation that have-nots experience when interacting with the national political processes can lead to the formation of strong identities and community solidarity, in particular where communities tend to be racially and culturally homogenous. Anthony Smith (1999) shows many nations are built on myths of common ancestry, historical memories, shared culture and a sense of solidarity. All of these factors bind together those who are 'of a nation'. Similarly, communities within a nation can also develop a sense of identity, and with that identity, a set of shared values are developed. Nationally, shared values may overlap strongly with democratic values, such as respect for the opinion of others, for reaching a negotiated consensus without conflict and abiding by the rule of law and society in all areas of human life. Communities within a nation may adhere to that broad framework while also developing their own values: rules by which their community operates. However, community norms can develop an insular character which leads them to view dominant national norms and cultures negatively.

Ashley Jardina's research hints at why communities facing the greatest challenges may be keen to form identities as well as protect the values that make them a community. Jardina (2019) argues that humans are primed to adopt group attachments: an identity. An identity is a psychological, internalised sense of attachment to a group which provides a cognitive structure that aids an individual to navigate their social and political environment. Threats to an identity lead to the development of protective mechanisms. Deprived areas may have a greater sense of internal co-operation to overcome hardships, but they may also develop mechanisms for excluding those they perceive to be outsiders. The more deprived and insular communities tend also to be more xenophobic and hostile to strangers. Jardina's research on American society demonstrates how over the last two decades, white racial solidarity has emerged as a response to the fear of the white American losing its majority, dominance and control. The perception of becoming a minority is traumatic: it represents a challenge to the historical absoluteness of white dominance. Within communities that have suffered worst during the economic crisis and longer-term restructuring of the American economy, there are higher levels of anger and disempowerment among the white working class. Jardina notes that as they have lost their social status with the decline of their industries, they have simultaneously come to feel outnumbered, disadvantaged and even oppressed. The fight back has involved the formation of a white racial solidarity that strives towards reasserting a racial order in which they retain or regain predominance and where those they feel to be the 'immigrants' are not given perceived greater privilege.

Under such circumstances, social norms evolve and develop a more non-inclusive and xenophobic character. Racial solidarity becomes a social norm, reflected in a discourse extoling the superiority of one race over others. Such exclusionary norms are borne out of lived experiences, community solidarity in the face of economic hardship and feelings of marginalisation. The lived experiences faced in these communities jar with the myths which explain the formation of American society and those feeling marginalised seek to understand the cause of the disconnect. The community solidarity and insularity lend themselves to blaming the outsider. As their position in society becomes threatened, they seek ways to counter the perceived injustices inflicted upon them. Jardina's research thus demonstrates how values, and the perceived causes of reality failing to meet values, form a basis for shaping social norms to which members of a community adhere and how by adhering to these norms the community is sustained. The conditions Jardina identifies are reflected within many communities which are more likely to mistrust elites and democratic institutions and so support right-wing, populist and nationalist parties.

Insularity is thus negative for democratic culture. It can mean an avoidance of opposing arguments and a weakening of respect for pluralism. Those who hold an insular perspective are likely to seek those of a similar view and show hostility to those who attempt to convince them to consider alternative perspectives. But values can evolve in more positive ways and lead to positive behaviours becoming normalised. Disgust at the polluting of the oceans with plastic has normalised for some an avoidance of unnecessary use of single-use plastic. Campaigners, such as those promoting environmentally friendly behaviour seek to make aberrant behaviour unacceptable. Their campaigns attempt to instil the belief that a majority of individuals support adherence to pro-environmental patterns of behaviour. Once there is a widespread view that a behaviour runs counter to societal norms, individuals will avoid such activities in order to prevent being judged negatively. Within environmental movements, opposition to democratic institutions can emerge, again due to feelings of disempowerment.

Social norms exist across a range of behaviours, and in particular when we consider tolerance of difference. Discriminatory language has long been considered to counter norms of democratic society and, at a minimum, be frowned upon and in some cases be punishable by law. Of course, those who hold racist, xenophobic or homophobic attitudes may not become more accepting or tolerant, however they may not vocalise their attitudes. Such a situation is not always good for societal cohesion. Suppressed attitudes can fester, lead to the formation of underground groups and result in more extreme forms of behaviour. Whether the attitudes being suppressed are those which are critical of governmental corruption or tolerance of difference, suppression is not without potential danger. If criticism of ideologies is suppressed, it prevents people speaking out, therefore disempowering them. It can also mean that alternative perspectives are not heard and a spiral of silence governs what can and cannot be voiced (Noelle-Neumann, 1974). A spiral of silence can take many forms, from attempts to suppress discrimination, hate speech or anti-democratic tendencies to the feeling that one should not disagree with a perceived majority. Just as one would not want to sit on the home benches wearing the scarf of the opposing football team, one might not admit to being anti-racist, pro-LGBTQ+ or anti-liberal if the prevailing mood is perceived to be against you.

Spirals of silence do not mean majoritarian norms go unchallenged. Those who hold strong values may well argue their case stridently. If the majoritarian view holds firm, as appears to have largely been the case with addressing the concerns raised by environmentalist campaigners since the 1970s, they might give up or develop negative views about the quality of democracy. The passion held, when met with unchanging practices and superficial or rhetorical address, may lead to strong and negative emotional reactions to the elites which they feel act as a barrier to greater environmental protection. Jardina's white Americans, suffering uncertainty as a result of economic restructuring and feeling overlooked, seem to be another group who have suffered due to majoritarian norms: in their case, the sovereignty of market forces over economic decisions. Their pleas to reject those norms and the policies that flow from them were ignored, and their experiences since have led them to become less trusting of institutions and weakened in their belief in the American dream mythology. These all lead them to be inward-looking and mistrusting of the outsider as well as the elite figures. As the communities changed, their values mutated.

## VALUES AND POLITICAL CHOICES

It is common to think of values as parts of human psychology which are learned at a formative age and which then persist through life; certainly early work in this field believed values and ideological positions were unchanging (see Converse, 1964). Sociologist Ronald Inglehart (1997) described this as the socialisation hypothesis. However, he argued that socialisation should not be divorced from social context and so suggested that values could also be learned as priorities are determined through life. In developing the scarcity hypothesis as complementary to socialisation, Inglehart argued that people 'value' most those things that are in short supply. These models of value development formed his explanation for how different generations hold different values.

Reflecting on the generation born in the 1930s and 1940s Inglehart found most born in these decades prioritised economic stability and national security as being at the core of the political platform of any would-be government. He explained this by the fact that these citizens were born in an era of economic depression and war, and so the privations experienced shaped the demands they made of their politicians throughout their lives. In contrast, the baby boomer generation, born in an era of affluence, but when the environment and global poverty emerged as key media tropes, were found to be more likely to prioritise values such as human rights, equality and ecological protection. Hence, he argued, differing generations developed quite contrasting world views and priorities.

Of course, context is not just related to the socio-economic circumstances experienced during formative years. The persistence of values may not make sense in a world where any communities' fortunes can change rapidly. Arguably a scarcity of jobs, economic security and prospects have significantly reoriented the values of working-class white Americans over recent decades, perhaps converting once outward facing baby boomers to be more insular and selfish in terms of the allocation of national resources. Inglehart would argue that this represents a shift to materialist values caused by a perceived and perhaps very real threat to the availability of the basic resources required for survival. He contrasts these to the post-materialist values held by more affluent communities. Arguably the extent to which an individual holds materialist or post-materialist values will significantly shape their view of the world, and in turn, determines which political parties, ideologies and positions they support.

Considering values on a spectrum, materialist and selfish on one end, post-materialist and benevolent on the other, is useful. We can imagine someone moving through life adjusting their perspectives in line with their experiences. Hence, rather than having fixed values, individuals and communities may move along the scale as they react to events. A person who in youth had been a fervent environmental and human rights campaigner may have kept those values as they started a family, but an economic crash may encourage them to put those values aside and prioritise policies that remedy the instability they face. Financial insecurity, mounting debt and job insecurity may shift that person further towards an insular and materialist set of values. In such a situation, caring for the environment is perceived to lack urgency and they join the campaign to re-open mines and drill for oil if these will directly and positively affect their livelihood. Similarly, an individual who supported multiculturalism and global mobility may favour a hostile environment for immigrants if they feel immigrant populations hinder them from having a secure job and ready access to public or social services.

Such values impact democracy because of the political projects that those who hold materialist or post-materialist values might support. Materialists are likely to reject projects that seek long term societal and global benefits in favour of policies that offer them immediate benefits. Due to the perceived threat to them from the pursuit of a post-materialist political agenda, they may see those policies as anathema to them and their adherents as the enemy. Where zero-sum choices emerge, pitting a materialist vision against its post-materialist counterpart, society becomes more polarised. Polarisation results from identities becoming interwoven with a political position that is driven by a set of normative values about how things ought to be. Each side develops the belief they are irrefutably correct and detractors therefore are irrefutably wrong. The emotional investment in 'your' side becomes stronger than any investment in broader concerns relating to democracy.

## THE CHALLENGE TO DEMOCRATIC STABILITY

The potential for changes in the values sketched out in the previous section is part of a wider context within which the values which sustain democracy are being eroded and supplanted by values which lead to the support for positions, ideologies and individuals which threaten social inclusivity and the ability to reach a negotiated consensus on how the nation should be governed. The cause has not been one single shock event, although one can point to terrorist attacks experienced widely across the world as one factor. However, a range of events led citizens to experience profound emotional responses that cumulatively diminish their respect for democracy's core principles, institutions and traditions. Colin Hay in his book 'Why we Hate Politics' (2007) charted how the declining power of governments in the face of global governance and business institutions had led to a weakening of ideologies and a focus on managerialism which undermined engagement with and participation in electoral politics. These long-term structural factors coupled with fluctuations in national and global economic fortunes, threats from terrorism and media that thrive more on the divisive and scandalous aspects of politics lead negative attitudes to develop about political institutions at every level.

The negative attitudes underpin a key area of concern for the health of democracies: the declining trust in political institutions across a range of nations (Dalton, 2014, p. 260). Declining trust does not immediately correspond to the issues that Hay identified, but to corollaries of the reduced power of the nation state to listen and respond to public concerns, all of which have led to the formation of a series of negative beliefs relating to politics. For example, less than 30% of US citizens believe politicians 'care' about citizens (Dalton, 2014, p. 261). Rather, politicians are believed to be cynical actors whose main objective is to obtain and retain power. Drawing on time-series data, Dalton observes a 34% decline in institutional confidence from 1960 to 2012 for most branches of the American state (Dalton, 2014, p. 263), the exception being the military. The non-governmental sector has not suffered the same decline, apart from the press, trust in which has declined from 29% to 9%. Similar attitudes, with some minor variances, are found in Germany (where citizens rate government and the legislature lowest for trust), France (where parties are awarded minimal trust) and the UK (Dalton, 2014, p. 264). While the claim that trust is at an all-time low in most Western societies may be an exaggeration, there is almost universal recognition that low trust is a problem for democracy.

The reason low trust is a problem is because of the values that shape trust. According to social scientist William Riker (2017), humans tend to trust those who have proven themselves to be honest, fair, transparent, able, benevolent and accountable. Increasingly, citizens appear to believe politicians' behaviour proves they should be distrusted; research suggests the widespread belief that politicians lie, are corrupt and evasive and are unwilling to take responsibility for mistakes. Politicians therefore are perceived to behave in ways that run counter to social norms; they are transgressive and so do not hold the same values as the non-politician.

## THE CHALLENGE OF POPULISM

The diminished trust in political institutions has paved the way for populist politicians. Populism has been described in terms of being a thin ideology based on the base fears and prejudices of sections of society: a political strategy that is designed to win support and a communicative style which involves making claims to speak as one with the people. The latter is perhaps the least detrimental to democracy. In fact, a number of scholars argue that support for populist politicians is encouraged due to the way they 'tell it like it is' and 'speak their mind' (Rooduijn, 2018). However, for many populists, 'telling it like it is' means abandoning politically correct language and argumentation and being exclusionary and discriminatory. As values change, as in white American industrial communities, populist discourse becomes normalized and shapes political preferences. The work of Cas Mudde (2016) demonstrates the link between changes in values, for example, in a Europe-wide poll where 85% of respondents agree that 'Nowadays there is too much tolerance', and in a rise in quite specific negative values which underpin Islamophobia and increased support for far-right movements such as Alternative for Deutschland/Sverige taking root. Recently, more mainstream parties such as current Conservative UK prime minister Boris Johnson, as well as Republican US President Donald Trump, have used Islamophobic language. The combination of shifts in values, terrorist attacks, economic crises and mistrust in mainstream politics leave a space for populist insurgents who are unrestrained by traditional norms to gain attention, claim to offer representation to those whom scholars refer to as the 'pure people' and combat the elites they so mistrust. Thus, populists tap into fears, propagate beliefs and change discourse. In the most extreme cases, populists exploit the human need to find meaning in the social order and make sense of shocking events using conspiracy theories. Conspiracy theories provide meaning and agency, one which removes guilt from the ordinary person. Often populists channel conspiracy theories to empower those whose agency is restricted by the proposed conspiracy (see Bergmann, 2018).

However, the typical strategy of the populist is to exploit the gap between how politicians interpret democratic values (the performance of representation) and the experiences of those who feel most marginalised in society. The 'have-nots' whose economic situations place them at the far end of the materialist spectrum, and who are most likely to have felt marginalised as progressive values have become normalised, have been the pioneers of a cultural backlash. Chiming with the work of Jardini, research by Ronald Inglehart and Pippa Norris found in a comparative study of nations that those who feel most threatened by economic uncertainty and cultural change are most likely to follow xenophobic, anti-elitist projects that engage in non-politically correct discourses. Their data leads them to suggest that

Less educated . . . citizens, especially white men, who were once the privileged majority culture in Western societies, resent being told that traditional values are 'politically incorrect' if they have come to feel that they are being marginalized within their own countries.

(Norris & Inglehart 2019, p. 29)

The greater levels of language that is deemed politically incorrect, or anti-democratic, leads in turn to a backlash from post-materialists who treat the less educated with disdain. Hillary Clinton's description of Trump supporters as a 'basket of deplorables' chimed with her supporters while contributing to the polarised nature of US politics during the 2016 presidential election and beyond. The societal polarisation which is both cause and consequence of the striking victories of Trump and the Brexit campaign in 2016 is highlighted as the outcome of societal inequalities and insecurities being channelled by populist rhetoric into voting decisions (Norris & Inglehart, 2019).

Russell Dalton (2014), based on data collected up to 2010, argued that we are "witnessing a transformation from social group cleavages to issue group cleavages" (p. 180). However, the rise of white identity politics and xenophobic nationalism challenges this post-materialist perspective of politics. Rather, we suggest, issue cleavages are most powerful and emotionally resonant when they become interconnected with identity cleavages. Divisions between the haves and have-nots have spilled over into questions of identity, and the questions of who should receive privilege within a society and who should be marginalised. We thus argue that as values become reconfigured due to economic insecurity, materialist values become more salient, making identity, community and social groups more important for those who feel threatened. The rapidly changing conditions of 21st century society leads to a situation where values may be constant, a product of socialisation, but for many might evolve and shift under the pressure of external factors. The uncertainty many experience drives adherence to materialist values which, combined with low trust, leads to a rise in anti-democratic tendencies.

At the heart of this analysis, however, is the recognition that emotional responses to lived experiences are key. While we should not defend xenophobic discourse and behaviour, we can understand the turn towards insularity. Many communities have suffered from de-industrialisation, making secure jobs a feature of history and giving way to temporary, zero-hour, unskilled labour which places people into poverty. If they feel marginalised, it is the fault of politicians for failing to reach a negotiated political consensus that meets the needs of these groups as well as economic interests. The disempowerment of these communities has been exploited by populists who seek to gain power by offering explanations and arguments that blame elites and outsiders. They offer agency through the ballot box and challenge the system which they blame for the plight of the ordinary people to whom they offer representation. Populists offer a powerful counter to dominant narratives and social norms, the power of which we explore in the next chapter.

## REFERENCES

Bergmann, E. (2018). *Conspiracy and populism: The politics of misinformation.* Palgrave Macmillan. https://doi.org/10.1007/978-3-319-90359-0

Converse, P. E. (1964). The nature of belief systems in mass publics. *Critical Review, 18*(1–3), 1–74. https://doi.org/10.1080/08913810608443650

Dalton, R. J. (2014). *Citizen politics: Public opinion and political parties in advanced industrial democracies.* CQ Press.

Hancock, A. M. (2016). *Intersectionality: An intellectual history.* Oxford University Press. https://doi.org/10.1093/acprof:oso/9780199370368.001.0001

Hay, C. (2007). *Why we hate politics.* Polity Press. https://doi.org/10.1017/S1537592708082194

Inglehart, R. (1997). *Modernization and postmodernization: Cultural, economic and political change in 43 societies.* Princeton University Press. https://doi.org/10.1086/210063

Jardina, A. (2019). *White identity politics.* Cambridge University Press. https://doi.org/10.1017/9781108645157

Mudde, C. (2016). *On extremism and democracy in Europe.* Routledge.

Noelle-Neumann, E. (1974). The spiral of silence a theory of public opinion. *Journal of Communication, 24*(2), 43–51. https://doi.org/10.1111/j.1460-2466.1974.tb00367.x

Norris, P., & Inglehart, R. (2019). *Cultural backlash: Trump, Brexit, and authoritarian populism.* Cambridge University Press. https://doi.org/10.1017/9781108595841

Riker, W. H. (2017). The nature of trust. In J. T. Tedeschi (Ed.), *Social power and political influence* (2nd ed., pp. 63–81). Routledge.

Rooduijn, M. (2018). What unites the voter bases of populist parties? Comparing the electorates of 15 populist parties. *European Political Science Review, 10*(3), 351–368. https://doi.org/10.1017/S1755773917000145

Smith, A. D. (1999). *Myths and memories of the nation.* Oxford University Press.

## FURTHER READING

Hancock, A. M. (2016). *Intersectionality: An intellectual history.* Oxford University Press. https://doi.org/10.1093/acprof:oso/9780199370368.001.0001

Inglehart, R. (1997) *Modernization and postmodernization: Cultural, economic and political change in 43 societies.* Princeton University Press. https://doi.org/10.1086/210063

Jardina, A. (2019). *White identity politics*. Cambridge University Press. https://doi.org/10.1017/9781108645157

Mudde, C. (2016). *On extremism and democracy in Europe*. Routledge.

Norris, P., & Inglehart, R. (2019). *Cultural backlash: Trump, Brexit, and authoritarian populism*. Cambridge University Press. https://doi.org/10.1017/9781108595841

# 2

---

# PROCESSING POLITICAL COMMUNICATION

As citizens, how we view ourselves, our role within society, our relationship with others and particularly the political system and how we understand that system is conditioned. Our education, experiences and the socioeconomic and political context all shape the narratives we tell and those we accept when explaining who we are and why we think the way we do. Although few nations actually condition their citizens, within most societies, some form of conditioning takes place. Conditioning is usually associated with the idea that our behaviour can be guided by triggers, as Pavlov proved by ringing a bell prior to giving his dog a treat; the conditioning meant every time the dog heard the bell it salivated looking forward to the treat. Perhaps advertising can have a similar effect, where we are led to buy products due to the expected benefits. In a political context, the use of advertising can represent a darker side of social control. The conditioning we experience relates to socialisation, the internalisation of social norms: the value and belief systems which make our community unique and offer us an identity. Sociologist Dalton Conley (2013) argues that our culture shapes us. If we understand culture to be the way history is uniformly taught in school and the references to our community in places of worship, through popular culture, political communication and media reports, then we can see how we can become socialised to adopt a perspective on the world provided that

DOI: 10.4324/9781003021292-2

the story we are told is consistent. Benignly, socialisation can help citizens conform to laws as well as acceptable norms of behaviour and to avoid stigmatisation, ostracism or punishment. Less benignly, citizens can be taught to believe a group to be an enemy of their community.

## SOCIALISATION AND DOMINANT NARRATIVES

What citizens learn depends on the dominant narratives within their society. A dominant narrative can be a grand meta-narrative, a story that defines a nation. The American dream fits well within the notion of a meta-narrative. It informs Americans that their future is in their hands, they can achieve anything they want through hard work and ambition. On the one hand, this should act as an encouragement to strive to follow one's dreams. But such a framework of understanding can lead to negative judgments being made about those who are trapped in poverty. The narrative of the American dream is thus powerful and is used by many candidates for political office as an explanation for their route from humble beginnings to the threshold of power. However, the American dream is also a myth, as many of the most powerful in America attain their wealth and status through inheritance and nepotism and those of non-white backgrounds are heavily disadvantaged. Yet, the narrative persists and was used as a counter argument to proposals by the Obama administration to introduce free health care. A statement by the conservative Tea Party group in 2010 argued the Patient Protection and Affordable Care Act represented "the most dangerous piece of legislation ever passed . . . as destructive to personal and individual liberties as the Fugitive Slave Act" (Economist, 2016). Opponents to what became known as Obamacare suggested that a person could only be free if they were entirely self-reliant. If a person relied on the state for health care, they owed a debt to the state and thus were enslaved. Just as a slave who had escaped the bonds of their owners was deemed to have earned their liberty once in a state where slavery was outlawed, and so earned self-determination, all Americans had the right to be free from state interference however benign. Hence, opposition to a system Europeans take for granted was positioned as inimical to the fundamentals of American society as the land of the free.

Dominant narratives do not have to be grand meta-narratives, however. They can be simpler and define the way in which the world operates. Neo-liberalism, the dominant economic theory of the late 20th and early 21st century explains the dominance of market forces and suggests it is impossible to buck or challenge the market. The value of goods and indeed the labour of an individual is determined by what the market will pay. Governments cannot save failing businesses as this represents an attempt to control market forces and would prove a waste of money as the market has already determined that business is unprofitable. Those who challenge such arguments, such as Trade Unions defending the jobs of their members, can find themselves labelled as being out of touch.

Other forms of dominant narratives are also constructed around the idea of the nation. British history is taught in such a way that glorifies the age of empire. The British Empire brought civilisation and wealth to the nations its empire encompassed; the exploitation and massacre of citizens of those nations is largely whitewashed from the official accounts (Dorling & Tomlinson, 2019). In contrast German history points to the dangers of disavowing one's history. School children are taught about Nazism and the Holocaust precisely to warn of the dangers of extremism and to encourage an awareness of the negative sides of nationalism. Thus, dominant narratives can be seen to have a range of effects on national identity. When used for political purposes the narratives at the heart of a national culture can strengthen beliefs in the norms they extol. At times of national crisis political leaders are wont to remind citizens of the shared national values. Similarly, during election campaigns citizens may be faced with competing perspectives on national values, with each candidate or party vying for election seeking to explain how their vision best evokes the character of the nation. Equally, they may argue how their manifesto adheres best to maintaining the values and social norms that hold a society together. However, within such contexts, dominant narratives can also act as a constraint. Mainstream parties tend not to deviate from the constraints imposed by a dominant narrative – most American presidential candidates attempt to situate their journey within the American dream trope; similarly, most parties develop their policies within a neo-liberal framework, intervening in market economics in limited ways. Hence, choices are limited and if dominant narratives are exposed as not serving citizens as a whole, their power can weaken. The weakening power of dominant narratives provides space for alternative narratives to gain traction.

## THE POWER OF COUNTERNARRATIVES

The global economic crisis of 2008 onwards was one moment that led many citizens to question the dominant interpretation of the world which they had been socialised to accept. The consensus around determined notions of how a society should be organised began to breakdown. With this breakdown, many centrist parties who had dominated their national political systems began to lose support. The effects were most dramatic for the centre-left parties of Greece and Spain. The Spanish PSOE, Socialist Workers Party, a dominant force from 1982, saw its parliamentary representation reduced from 96 to 54 seats from 2008–11, with further declines in support in 2015 and 2016, the frequency of elections demonstrating the increasing instability of Spain's democracy in this period. In Greece, the Panhellenic Socialist Movement (PASOK) was eclipsed by the leftish populist SYRIZA coalition led by the charismatic Alexis Tsipras, leading to a dramatic reorientation of the party system. This was not simply a feature of nations with somewhat shorter democratic histories. The impact of the crisis saw the political landscape change in a variety of countries. New parties with more radical platforms gained power, some emerging from grassroots movements others presenting themselves as being the authentic voice of the people. Such parties and candidates rejected the narrow framework citizens believed explained the socio-economic and political conditions of their nation. Citizens began to question their adherence to the norms that led them to offer support to the centrist consensus and sought alternatives.

However, in many nations the austerity measures shifted norms further. In some nations there was a rise in support for left-wing populist politics. Self-styled socialist Bernie Sanders gained a significant following in the Democrat primaries in 2016 and 2020, a significant departure for American politics. Elsewhere the rise to power of SYRIZA in Greece and the Labour party in New Zealand led by Jacinda Ardern, and the growth of support for Podemos in Spain and the UK Labour Party which had moved left under the leadership of Jeremy Corbyn, suggested that an anti-equality and anti-austerity programme had electoral credibility. However, globally, it seemed that competing counternarratives gained greater traction. Trump's election in the US in 2016, the success of the campaign to leave the EU in the UK, and increased votes for right wing parties across the European Union showed that a more isolationist and nationalist narrative resonated more within have-not communities (as discussed in the previous chapter). It was a narrative that also resonated with the older home-owning middle classes, a major Trump supporter demographic, who perceive themselves to have lost their status within a world where the values are very different to the ones they were socialised in.

A number of further counternarratives remained peripheral. Pro-environmentalist narratives, and narratives tackling the inequalities relating to intersectionality seem to have been in turn pushed down the public agenda. On the one hand, we found counternarratives having impact on the broader public mood. Michael Bamberg and Molly Andrews (2004) argued that as counternarratives gain traction they become micro-discursive accomplishments, giving voice to groups who do not subscribe to the hegemonic narrative while also having an impact on the evolution of public values. As values change, the average position of a society on the Overton window, the range of policies politically acceptable to the mainstream population at a given time, can also change. Naturally not all counternarratives have any significant impact. Although, they can gain traction within small communities which can create a micro public sphere which in turn can form the basis for a social movement. The formation of such groups has challenged some of the gender inequalities within Arab societies without challenging the overarching societal structures (Elsheikh & Lilleker, 2019). Normally, a society where hegemonic narratives can be challenged is generally seen as a well-functioning and pluralist democracy as it allows for open debate on the policies and issues of the day as well as the underpinning values that set parameters for policy. This view of society presupposes the existence of the conditions for a public sphere, those being the existence of politically active and informed citizens, open communicative spaces, a free and pluralist media, and a tradition of deliberation (Habermas, 1989). However, the Covid-19 pandemic has largely seen a single narrative being disseminated via traditional media, with alternative perspectives censored even on social media and free speech and critical thinking suppressed. While one can argue that in the interests of public safety, and indeed the interests of future generations when climate change deniers are not given a voice in media, the suppression of counter-narratives is consistent with the best interests of society, such practices can undermine the principles of democracy and the cohesion of society.

Those who protest censorship on the grounds of free speech have a wider effect on how citizens feel about the way society is governed. Those whose concerns are not given voice, independent of the perceived rationality of their arguments, can find audiences among those who have heightened anxiety and low trust in institutions. Often, those who feel unrepresented are also disengaged from politics so are most likely to be uninformed and inactive. If they talk about public affairs, it is likely to be within insular online spaces, particularly during lockdowns. These citizens may also access a narrow diet of media. Hence, rather than pluralism, one gets polarisation, which if effective encourages those excluded to feel empowered as critical thinkers versus a majority whose thinking is controlled. During the pandemic, narratives emerged where those who believed the pandemic was not as serious as claimed by governments were lions whereas those obeying the rules were sheep. The challenge for democracy is that these have-nots feel unrepresented and excluded by dominant narratives but the only counternarratives are polarising and anti-democratic. Citizens who are most likely to fall into the have-not category, with lower levels of education, high economic insecurity and low political knowledge and engagement, are also those most likely to believe in conspiracy theories which offer metanarratives of covert and clandestine plots that create inequalities, subvert democratic practices and pit the good people versus evil elites. Hence, if the mechanisms for building traction for counternarratives involve employing tales of conspiracies and xenophobic and exclusionary language, this can polarise society and inhibit open debate. Such negative trends, which are visible in many countries and have been exacerbated during the pandemic, lead adherents of either side of the divide to retreat to media, communities and spaces where views are largely homogenous and where their values are not challenged.

## POLITICAL COMMUNICATION

It is widely recognised that politics follow the character of a permanent campaign. Elected presidents and governments do not just inform citizens but sell their policies as being the best. Opposition parties highlight the weaknesses of the approach of those who govern, sometimes promoting alternative courses of action. Centrist or mainstream parties will likely fit their communication within the dominant narrative, offering alternative interpretations of the course of action that best fits to the shared values of the nation. Outside of parliaments, a range of non-governmental organisations, charities and pressure or protest groups vie for the attention of the media and citizenry in order to advance their causes. These non-electoral groups may also promote the dominant narrative; however, these may also provide the source for a range of counternarratives. Political persuasion is hence an all-pervasive part of the daily life of citizens living in democracies. The way citizens engage with communication and its impact on their thinking is detailed in the next chapter, here however, we consider what cognitive filter mechanisms may be in operation.

Citizens with a rich diet of media, accessing multiple sources of television and newspaper news while also accessing news websites, weblogs and being exposed to political news, views and opinions on social media may be overloaded with competing interpretations and ideas. Unless they belong to that small elite who are highly engaged consumers of political news, they need to decide which sources to listen to, which views are most valid and so which political programme offers the best outcomes for them. The danger for democracies is that filtering systems can lead to errors of judgment caused by the cognitive shortcuts used as filters or the information networks which citizens inhabit. The latter being how restricted their diet of news is, how reliant they are on a single source and the credibility of that source, as well as the extent that they willingly expose themselves to a range of diverse and competing viewpoints. Hence, we consider the role of some of the major theories which explain how information is cognitively filtered to raise questions about the extent that citizens are well-informed and engage with pluralist debates.

## CONFIRMATION BIAS

Confirmation bias simply explains how persuasive messages have greater power if they confirm a position we already believe. Research shows that any piece of communication is assessed according to two fairly instantaneously registered pieces of information. Firstly, what is the piece of communication and secondly, what are our assumptions and expectations about it (Lord & Taylor, 2009)? The way confirmation bias works can be illustrated with an example. During the 2019 UK election campaign, British Prime Minister Boris Johnson was interviewed by BBC political journalist, Andrew Marr. Marr and Johnson frequently talked over each other and showed little respect for one another. At one stage Marr said: "you just keep going on and on – you are chuntering"; Johnson responding, "you are interrupting if I may say so. I think people might be quite interested in my answers as well as your questions". Zoe Williams writing in the left-wing newspaper The Guardian described the 28-minute conversation as "at least, democratically and impartially, horrible for everyone to watch – staccato, over-enunciated, hostile, hard to follow" (Williams, 2019). The interview attracted 12,172 complaints from members of the audience; some felt Johnson's 'untruths' were insufficiently challenged, others thought Marr was disrespectful and antagonistic (BBC, 2019). How did significant numbers of people watching the same interview arrive at such different conclusions? Using confirmation bias to explain this, we hypothesise that audience members interpreted the interview according to their previously held assumptions about the BBC or about prime minister Johnson. According to a recent YouGov poll conducted in December 2019, 54% of people who supported the Conservative Party in 2017 did not fully trust BBC News journalists to tell the truth, compared to 49% and 33% of 2017 Labour and Liberal Democrat voters, respectively (Ibbetson, 2019). So those who supported Johnson were likely to feel he was due respect, and the BBC was likely to be biased against him, resulting in the confrontational style adopted in the interview. Johnson's detractors viewed him as someone who obfuscated and lied and so deserving of tough interrogation. So very simply, the audience demonstrated selective attention to aspects of the interview based on their feelings towards Johnson and the presenter. Conservative Party supporters who did not trust the BBC presenter favoured Johnson over Marr. On the other hand, Labour and Liberal Democrat voters who may not trust Marr or Johnson accused Marr of being too soft and not sufficiently challenging the Prime Minister.

Differential interpretations were also offered by a number of news sources the following day. The Conservative supporting Daily Express, for instance, offered the interpretation in their headline on the day after the interview, that "Viewers write complaints to BBC about Marr as he 'loses temper' in Boris Johnson interview" (Harris, 2019). In contrast, William (2019) in the left-wing Guardian, while admitting Marr was rude, her editorial stated "Johnson did deliver numerous untruths, and they were allowed to lie there like fish out of their bowl, flapping on the floor until they died". The partisanship of the newspapers, and their readers, thus coloured their interpretation of the interview. The Daily Express, as a newspaper supportive of the Conservatives, produced an editorial that reflected the bias of its readership; likewise, the Guardian confirmed their readers' likely interpretation of Marr as the frustrated interrogator unable to counter Johnson's misleading claims. Each narrative plays to the potential bias of its audience, reinforcing its own interpretations of a highly combative interview drawing on partisan perspectives.

Confirmation bias has been extensively studied by psychologists and is defined as the seeking or interpreting of evidence in ways that conform to existing beliefs, expectations or explanatory hypotheses (Nickerson, 1998, p. 175). It is thus suggested that when new information is received, not often all the information is fully absorbed, rather bits of data are selected and only the bits which reinforce our existing prejudices. Thinking about the Marr-Johnson interview, a left-wing Guardian reader may not consider the acceptance that Marr was rude to Johnson but the elaborate reference to his lies may be the part that is selected as being important. If a Conservative supporter read the same piece, Marr's rudeness may stand out and the comment about the lies be dismissed as partisan bias and hyperbole. Confirmation bias works across a range of socio-political contexts and alongside partisan preference, our gender, ethnicity, educational and socioeconomic backgrounds and lifestyles all shape our prejudices and expectations (Nickerson, 1998, p. 182).

As hinted at when discussing the different media interpretations of Johnson's interview, many citizens are also selective with respect to where they get information. Media choices are argued to be led by a desire for affirmation as opposed to information, research consistently shows that people prefer to believe propositions we desire to be true over those we hope are false. Studies in the field of psychology demonstrate that people find being proven correct easier to deal with, as largely no-one likes to be told they are wrong. Consequently, there is a tendency to seek information sources that confirm beliefs (Koslowski & Maqueda, 1993, p. 104). In the case of Johnson's interview with Marr, a Conservative Party supporter who thought Johnson was excessively challenged by the BBC presenter would have preferred to read sources such as the Daily Express, which are known for supporting the Conservative Party and would provide evidence consistent with their interpretation of the confrontation. In contrast, the anti-Johnson Guardian reader wants their view of Johnson misleading the audience reinforced and prefers the perception of the BBC as frustrated or even cowed by his evasive or erroneous responses.

However, a range of other biases can be evidenced, many of which are harmful to the principles of pluralism that underpin democracy. Biases regarding the privileges awarded one race, religion, gender or sexual orientation are often played upon to accentuate the position of one party over another. Since the terrorist attacks on the New York World Trade Centre towers on 9/11 in 2001 and subsequent attacks on the transport networks in Madrid and London as well as various atrocities including on attendees at the Bataclan nightclub in Paris and Manchester Arena in the UK have led to increasing suspicion of and demonisation of Muslims. The acceptance of mostly Muslim refugees from Syria by the German government, and numerous disputable stories about their anti-social behaviour circulating on social media platforms, has been exploited by the far-right Alternative für Deutschland (AfD) to gain representation in the Reichstag. The suggestion that 76 million Turkish Muslims could be allowed to enter the UK 'when' Turkey joins the EU was a highly contestable statement used as part of the argument for the UK leaving the EU in 2016. The fears of Islamification of European societies fuelled support for the Eurabia conspiracy theory which suggests that EU leaders and leftist actors are complicit in allowing Islamic cultures and traditions to gain a protected and eventually a dominant position. The threat posed was documented in an extensive manifesto released online by Anders Breivik the day in 2011 he attacked the office of the Norwegian prime minister and shot dead 69 members of the Norwegian Labour Party youth movement on Utøya island (Bergmann, 2018). Similar conspiracy theories fuelled Brenton Tarrant's attack on a mosque in Christchurch, New Zealand in 2019. Conspiracy theories regarding 'a great reset' have also circulated during the pandemic, with groups such as QAnon claiming the existence of a plot to give governments greater control over citizens by enforcing lockdowns and controlling information. While extreme examples, such events are resultant from the phenomenon of confirmation bias where adherents of a conspiracy theory develop a psychosis.

Chiming with the work of Carolyn Sherif et al. (1981) confirmation bias is at the heart of social judgement theory. According to this theory, a recipient weighs new information against their existing point of view to determine whether it should be accepted or rejected. Where the individual is uncommitted on an issue, the source may be influential. An individual might find someone trying to persuade them as more credible if they deem them to be highly similar. This assessment can be made on racial, gender, ethnic or sexuality grounds. Alternatively, it can be a judgment about the persuaders' authenticity. Many seeking election emphasise both their expertise as well as their normalcy. Populists, in particular, emphasise that they are non-elites who represent the 'pure people' in a conflict against elites. Campaign groups also appear highly successful when they have a figurehead who can mobilise certain social groups; the effect of Swedish teenager Greta Thunberg in building a global movement of young people is perhaps as much a reflection of her similarity to the people who support her as her passion and defiant argumentation.

All of this demonstrates that humans are not always rational creatures, and confirmation bias can even be found among elite decision makers. The historian Barbara Tuchman found that, despite being against its interests, the US military stayed in Vietnam for 16 years. Tuchman argued that once a policy has been adopted and implemented by a government, all subsequent activity of that government becomes focused on the justification of that policy. This phenomenon is explained, again, by the human innate desire to be right (De Wit, 2018, p. 67) as well as the phenomenon that, through a process of building a justification for a policy, belief of correctness hardens and those involved develop tunnel vision. In the case of the Vietnam, military advisors and politicians disregarded information about negative progress and concentrated on arguments that supported their presence in the Vietnam War and sought refuge in the scant evidence that they would win. Being right is so important that we might even convince ourselves that every source of evidence which counters our beliefs is false, even when the evidence is incontrovertible. We can see this in a more recent case: US President Donald Trump and his

rhetorical war against the media. Trump dismisses all negative headlines in the media about his presidency as "fake" or "phony"; this has
accelerated to the point where Trump decries as "fake" every source
of information besides himself on his Twitter account (Keith, 2018).
Even criticisms of his handling of the Covid-19 pandemic have been
called fake and partisan, with him branding the World Health Organisation as at fault for not clearly informing the world about the threat
of the virus and being insufficiently interrogative of data from China
where the virus strain originated.

Along with these motivating factors, there are also cognitive factors that play a role in producing conformation bias. Psychological research has shown that people are fundamentally limited to
thinking about only one subject at a time and, after having focused
on a particular hypothesis, that hypothesis dominates their interpretation. Even regarding that single hypothesis, they are more
inclined to assume that the statement is more true than false, but
not to consider alternative interpretations. Hence, populists are able
to convince people of the dangers of immigration (restricting the
availability of school places, housing and access to health services)
as opposed to the benefits of a vibrant multicultural society. It is
also shown that when people are asked to generate explanations,
they express greater confidence in their own explanation (Koehler,
1991). During a rally in El Paso in 2019, former President Trump
actively used this cognitive bias in his communication strategy.
Despite no sign of construction commencing on the promised wall
between Mexico and the US, Trump changed his campaign slogan
from 'Build the Wall' to 'Finish the Wall' and explained why the wall
needed to be finished (Olorunnipa et al., 2019). With this shift in
emphasis, Trump urged his supporters to imagine the possibility of
a wall under construction. If a Trump supporter was then asked to
explain why the wall needed to be finished, they would be required
to think that the construction of the wall had started and would try
to explain why the wall had to be completed. Psychological studies
have shown that even though a person could later be informed about
the truth, they would be more 'likely', in this case, to consider the

wall's construction as having started than others who were not asked to explain why it might not have started (Ross, 1977). This suggests that directing people to focus on one of several possible outcomes increases the subjective likelihood of supporting the privileged outcome (Nickerson, 1998). Other empty slogans such as 'Get Brexit Done' or 'Make America Great Again' suggest a journey started that can only be completed by the individual rhetorician. By suggesting a process is incomplete and requires a conclusion directs the voter to award the architect of the phrase, and of course the process, their support to finish that job.

It is important to highlight here that such processes are natural. Humans are pragmatists and their cognitive processes are organised in such a way as to minimise costly errors (Friedrich, 1993). For example, after being burned by touching a flame, it is safer to assume that all fires will harm us. It is often the same in politics, in that we often 'know' in advance what we are going to like and what we are going to dislike based on the values and beliefs that we acquire through socialisation processes. We are more concerned with making the right decisions and so assess which outcome will have the least harmful consequences for us personally and as a community. If we do not approve of a particular policy of a political party, it is often safe to assume that we will also not like their future policies. Instead of being experimental and trying different options, we stick with the knowledge we know and make generalisations. A similar process occurs with information selection. Psychological studies reveal that, if we see biased news that is against our beliefs and values, this creates the uncomfortable feeling of cognitive dissonance (De Wit, 2018). Thinking that all information will be biased, we avoid looking at the news source in question, so avoiding future dissonance. We thus might try to retreat into 'echo chambers', a metaphor used to explain how citizens limit their exposure only to opinions that correspond to their those they already hold (Sunstein, 2001). The widespread usage of social media has made the concept of echo chambers a relevant topic of scholarly debate.

## ECHO CHAMBERS AND INFORMATION CASCADES

We accept Bruns's (2019) argument that it is impossible to filter out all competing views and opinions, but that is possible to avoid receiving a purely pluralist and balanced diet of information and that confirmation bias can determine the credibility of information. The 21st century hypermedia environment offers significant opportunities to tailor the information received to specific topics of interest and limit obtaining multiple points of view. The Internet allows us to bypass so-called mainstream sources and engage with different types of opinions and analyses. In turn, social media algorithms show us content similar to that we frequently engage with, hence, certain information sources may be prioritized in news feeds due to the number of likes or shares they are awarded by us or our close network peers.

Hence, the increasingly open but customizable structure of the Internet has proven to be a double-edged sword. Although citizens can use the online environment to expand their horizons, it is also easy in this unregulated space to find sources that share our views and interests and confirm our beliefs. While traditional media present topics and points of view that we cannot select ourselves, the Internet offers the opportunity for any user to narrow their information diet to websites, platforms, users or messages that are particularly tailored to match their own interests and prejudices. Instead of transforming ourselves into globally informed citizens, we may end up creating a "Daily Me" (Sunstein, 2001).

Recently, Bakshy et al. (2015) analysed the Facebook activities of 10.1 million active US users. They tested what determined the type of information these users encountered on Facebook and found that what those users encountered on social media depended on who their friends were and what information they shared. In their sample, users had more than 20% of friends from an opposing ideological viewpoint. Accordingly, the users had the potential for being exposed to opposing views of different sources. But when Barsky et al. analysed the extent to which users were exposed to opposing views, they found liberals tended to have fewer friends who shared information that contrasted their own (24% of the news shared was crosscutting) compared to their conservative counterparts (35% of the news shared were crosscutting). An important point indicated in this research is that, although Facebook users were exposed to opposing views on social media, their social media network was mainly composed of like-minded people. This is significant, as social psychology studies show that when we "lack independent information sources, we will often rely on information provided by the statements or actions of others around us" (Sunstein, 2001, p. 10). This can lead to a cascade effect, in which information is spread from one person to another with the ultimate result that a large number of people believe something simply because others seem to believe it too (Sunstein, 2001). This phenomenon can prove powerful for the propagation of any form of content, from those promoting democratic participation, championing environmentalist campaigns, combatting xenophobia or spreading conspiracy theories.

A good example of this cascade effect is the case of the United Kingdom Independence Party (UKIP) and its transformation into an increasingly hard-right, populist force between 2018 and 2019. It was seen that the emergence of a large number of angry, young and tech-savvy far-right UKIP supporters was not only linked to party members but also to far-right YouTubers and online news sites such as Kipper Central, Politicalite.com and Unity News, which were heavily supportive of the hard-line agenda of then leader Gerard Batten. Unity News attracted more than 120,000 users a month and disseminated messages supporting the party's agenda, propagating terms such as "the biased media" (Halliday & Walker, 2019). Online discussion amongst this group of UKIP supporters spread the criticism of the British media and reinforced negative beliefs about an anti-Brexit media elite, particularly focusing their critique on the BBC. Their label of traitor was levelled at any groups which contested Brexit, leading to a highly polarised atmosphere.

Hence, to return to the analysis of the Johnson and Marr interview, we can assert that the opinions of citizens who watched the interview might also have been affected by the people who inhabit their social media network. If these citizens' social media networks are mostly formed of like-minded friends and family members, they would not only be affected by their previous assumptions, but also by predilections and prejudices circulating in their network. Thus, there are numerous ways that confirmation bias undermine the pluralist principles on which democracies operate and lead to the rise of extremist views and polarisation within our societies.

## SOCIETAL POLARISATION IN THE DIGITAL AGE

While political polarisation is not purely a feature of what we might term the digital age, or indeed only prevalent in nations with a high penetration of social media platform usage, polarisation is argued to be accelerated due to digital platforms. Social psychology studies have revealed that engaging in discussion in online communities acts a significant source of confirmation bias, it can also contribute to polarisation as beliefs are strengthened. Being a part of a community leads to the formation of a collective identity which can lead to conformity and lead members to adopt more extreme political positions. Due to personal and group identities becoming blurred, a loyalty develops that leads members to be reluctant to question the dominant group narrative. This phenomenon leads to effective polarisation with society divided not just on ideological lines but on identities which can have wider political ramifications. Research showed high levels of homogeneity and a hardening of attitudes within pro-Brexit communities in the UK during the referendum campaign (Lilleker & Bonacci, 2017); subsequently, those opposing Brexit have been labelled traitors, while all those in favour are seen as stupid or racist. Such perspectives mean the two sides are unable to talk to one another. Political communication has been seen as important here in manipulating the emotions which drive excitement for a political outcome and anxiety that the outcome is under threat. Such propagandistic devices have proven successful for driving support for extremist Islamic perspectives (Baines et al., 2010) but clearly have wider applications within political campaigning. If communities form around such beliefs, the emotions drive attitudes which are strengthened. As community members seek to avoid the feeling of dissonance, they will become more extreme in their opinions and they develop more extreme attitudes in order to fit in with the wider group.

Apart from the composition of social media networks, platform algorithms can also influence whether a citizen is likely to encounter information that confirms their views and drives more extreme attitudes. Algorithms are coded instructions which influence the flow of information across individual news feeds on social media platforms. They are often comprised of a history of likes, comments and shares that direct the algorithmic engine. As the content we encounter is mostly selected on the basis of our previous behaviour, scholars warn that this might lead to 'filter bubbles', wherein we only encounter information we have previously chosen (Bakshy et al., 2015). The hardening of attitudes that can occur as existing beliefs are confirmed, particularly within an intense political campaign, can further contribute to societal polarisation across competing extreme attitudes.

Individual users are not alone in influencing the platforms' algorithmic engines. Platform owners can also direct user relationships, experiences and the contents on these channels by tweaking the platforms' algorithms. Recently, for instance, digital media scholar Zeynep Tufekci (2018) realised that when she watched Donald Trump rallies on YouTube during the 2016 campaign, the platform recommended and auto-played videos for her that featured white supremacist speeches. She then observed that every time she consulted moderately right-wing content, the platform recommended more extreme content. While such extremist content helps site-owners attract audiences to the platform, due to its attractiveness, such content further impacts the pluralist nature of societal discourse. During the early months of the pandemic, similar dynamics were at play. Confirmation bias, coupled with the human natural aversion to content that conflicts their views, and their reliance on heuristics, thus means that the social media environment can have highly deleterious effects on the health of our democracy. This argument is developed further as we consider how individuals engage cognitively with political communication.

## REFERENCES

Baines, P. R., O'Shaughnessy, N. J., Moloney, K., Richards, B., Butler, S., & Gill, M. (2010). The dark side of political marketing: Islamist propaganda, reversal theory and British Muslims. European Journal of Marketing, 44(3–4), 478–495. https://doi.org/10.1108/03090561011020543

Bakshy, E., Messing, S., & Adamic A. L. (2015). Exposure to ideologically diverse news and opinion on Facebook. Political Science, 348(6239), 1130–1132. https://doi.org/10.1126/science.aaa1160

Bamberg, M., & Andrews, M. (2004). Considering counter-narratives: Narrating, resisting, making sense. John Benjamins Publishing. https://doi.org/10.1075/sin.4

BBC. (2019). Andrew Marr's interview with Boris Johnson attracts 12,000 complaints. https://www.bbc.co.uk/news/entertainment-arts-50778240

Bergmann, E. (2018). Conspiracy and populism: The politics of misinformation. Palgrave Macmillan. https://doi.org/10.1007/978-3-319-90359-0

Bruns, A. (2019). Are filter bubbles real? John Wiley & Sons.

Conley, D. (2013). You may ask yourself: An introduction to thinking like a sociologist. W.W. Norton & Company.

De Wit, L. (2018). What's your bias?: The surprising science of why we vote the way we do. Elliott & Thompson Ltd.

Dorling, D., & Tomlinson, S. (2019). Rule Britannia: BREXIT and the end of empire. Biteback Publishing.

Economist (2016) Why Republicans hate Obamacare. https://www.economist.com/the-economist-explains/2016/12/11/why-republicans-hate-obamacare

Elsheikh, D., & Lilleker, D. G. (2019). Egypt's feminist counterpublic: The re-invigoration of the post-revolution public sphere. New Media & Society, 23(1), 22–38. https://doi.org/10.1177/1461444819890576

Friedrich, J. (1993). Primary error detection and minimization (PEDMIN) strategies in social cognition: A reinterpretation of confirmation bias phenomena. *Psychological Review*, 100(2), 298–319. https://doi.org/10.1037/0033-295x.100.2.298

Habermas, J. (1989). *The structural transformation of the public sphere: An inquiry into a category of bourgeois society*. The MIT Press.

Halliday, J., & Walker, P. (2019, March 3). UKIP 2.0: Young, angry, digital and extreme. *The Guardian*. https://bit.ly/2FskCMp

Harris, K. (2019, December 2). Viewers write complaints to BBC about Marr as he "loses temper" in Boris Johnson interview. *The Daily Express*. https://bit.ly/2SXp4ef

Ibbetson, C. (2019, December 16). Do Briton trust the press. *YouGov*. https://bit.ly/2rZ2Tcq

Keith, T. (2018, September 2). President Trump's description of what's "fake" is expanding. *National Public Radio*. https://n.pr/2T1INcD

Koehler, D. (1991). Explanation, imagination and confidence in judgement. *Psychological Bulletin*, 110(3), 499–519. https://doi.org/10.1037/0033-2909.110.3.499

Koslowski, B., & Maqueda, M. (1993). What is confirmation bias and when do people actually have it? *Merrill-Palmer Quarterly*, 39(1), 104–130.

Lilleker, D. G., & Bonacci, D. (2017). The structure of political e-expression: What the Brexit campaign can teach us about political talk on Facebook. *International Journal of Digital Television*, 8(3), 335–350.

Lord, G. C., & Taylor, A. C. (2009). Biased assimilation: Effects of assumptions and expectations on the interpretation of new evidence. *Social and Personality Psychology Compass*, 3(5), 827–841. https://doi.org/10.1111/j.1751-9004.2009.00203.x

Nickerson, R. (1998). Confirmation bias: A ubiquitous phenomenon in many guises. *Review of General Psychology*, 2(2), 175–220. https://doi.org/10.1037/1089-2680.2.2.175

Olorunnipa, T., Costa, R., & Dawsey, J. (2019, February 16). "Finish that wall": Trump seeks to turn his failure to build the wall into campaign rallying cry. *Washington Post*. https://wapo.st/2QtuJHj

Ross, L. (1977). The intuitive psychologist and his shortcomings. In L. Berkowitz (Ed.), *Advances in experimental social psychology* (pp. 173–220). Academic Press. https://doi.org/10.1016/S0065-2601(08)60357-3

Sherif, C., Sherif, M., Nebergall, R. (1981). Attitude and Attitude Change: the social judgment-involvement approach. New York: Greenwood Press.

Sunstein, C. (2001). *Echo chambers*. Princeton University Press.

Tufekci, Z. (2018, March 10). YouTube: The greater radicaliser. *The New York Times*. www.nytimes.com/2018/03/10/opinion/sunday/youtube-politics-radical.html

Williams, Z. (2019). Chuntering and untruths: why Andrew Marr's interview with Boris Johnson was so controversial. The Guardian. https://www.theguardian.com/media/shortcuts/2019/dec/03/chuntering-and-untruths-why-andrew-marrs-interview-with-boris-johnson-was-so-controversial

## FURTHER READING

Bergmann, E. (2018). *Conspiracy and populism: The politics of misinformation*. Palgrave Macmillan. https://doi.org/10.1007/978-3-319-90359-0

Lilleker, D. G. (2014). *Political communication and cognition*. Palgrave Macmillan.

Sanborn, F. W., & Harris, R. J. (2013). *A cognitive psychology of mass communication*. Routledge.

# 3

---

# THINKING ABOUT POLITICS

Having introduced the citizen as an emotionally driven creature and discussed how they develop their political perspectives and how this governs their evaluation of political communication, this chapter delves a little deeper. Here we explore and explain what psychological factors determine how citizens engage with political communication. More importantly, we enquire how citizens form judgements about political messages but also about political actors. According to economic models, when faced with political information, individuals follow normative theories of logic: a slow, deliberative process that relies on rules and calculations. Yet, psychologists such as Kahneman (2011) and Gigerenzer (2008) remind us that we often systematically and predictably deviate from these norms. Individuals often choose routinized thinking that is quicker and based on heuristics and biases. Certain words, images or other presentational cues, as we shall see, might lead to forming quick judgments about the relevance, credibility and importance of an item of political communication.

In this chapter, we refer to proximity and valence theories. The proximity principle concerns the tendency for individuals to form interpersonal relationships with those who are deemed familiar. Here, we can relate back to social judgment and why a source can make a message more acceptable due to perceived or actual similarity. Proximity theory argues that physical and psychological 'nearness' to

DOI: 10.4324/9781003021292-3

others tends to increase interpersonal persuasion. During the 2011 uprisings, for example, leaders within the governorates and districts of Egypt attempted to mobilise the neighbourhoods that they represented, using their localism to reinforce their messages. The more we see of a person, the more we feel close to that person. Hence, authoritarian leaders try to create a cult around the authenticity of their personality and their charismatic ordinariness to build and maintain support.

Relevant, or valent, messages are also judged to have greater credibility. The leaders of Egyptian protests spoke directly about the experiences of the people they represented, drawing on their knowledge of the problems within specific districts and neighbourhoods. Hence, both source proximity and message valence are shown to influence the persuasiveness of messages. These theories show how big data is used to assist politicians to construct arguments that match their target audience's values and beliefs and lead them to consider arguments carefully, what we refer to here as deep cognition.

However, proximity and valence are not everything. Just one part of a message can be sufficient to impact a person's attitudes and political engagement. Individuals might be interested in the message of the political actor they perceive as most competent, as in the case of Trump and his working-class supporters. This chapter therefore examines the power the simple images and slogans used in widely in political communication have. Such simple communication has a memetic quality, because it can be disseminated widely and can gain traction via digital platforms. Here, we highlight the power of political communication that has a heuristic quality, and how it can have influence on voters' choices. We particularly contextualise this discussion within the digital age, where technology provides a whole range of opportunities for political actors to influence citizens. The fast-moving, fragmented and crowded information environment provides spaces where exposure to heuristics can build perceptions. Drawing on schema theory, we discuss the problems we can find in the hybrid media environment including the potential power of 'fake news'.

## WHY POLITICAL JUDGMENTS MAY NOT BE LOGICAL

If you have not come across this question before, please test yourself. If a bat and ball costs £1.10 and the bat costs £1 more than the ball, how much is the ball? If you said 5 pence you are correct and you have either been asked this before or you are among the 20% of average citizens who are consistently carefully considering every question posed. If you answered 10 pence, relax, you are in the majority, but beware it means you are more susceptible to being manipulated. This is not to claim that 80% of people are generally gullible. Those who answer 10 pence may not care, they are not in the shop, they are not buying a ball, and so give no importance to the question. Answering 10 pence shows that when considering the question, there was minimal cognitive engagement and instead you were tricked into giving the answer that seemed most obvious.

What about an alternative question? 'Is it fair we house immigrants while our veterans sleep on the streets? Click like to say no'. Imagine this on your social media feed. Many may feel there is an inherent injustice that those who served the country, and possibly suffer with mental health as a result, are not prioritised above outsiders to the community. These people will click like and the message gains traction. Others will recognise that the tragedy of homelessness among veterans is not simply due to there being insufficient housing, or because immigrants are given priority. These will see the link made in the message as misleading and the post as manipulative, they will not click like and they might report it. However, as with the question about the bat and the ball, it requires greater concentration to realise the problem with this message.

It may not seem important that people are sometimes beguiled by manipulative communication, however that is not the case. In fact, there are two dangers inherent with being beguiled in the digital age. Firstly, those who click like are not sending a message to any department of government which might impact their housing policies, but they may be giving a far-right activist group permission to see their social media profile, gather data and contact them. Secondly, not only might the original recipient remember the message, but by clicking like, they may also make the image more visible within their online network. Moreover, clicking like could act as a gateway to seeing similar, more extreme content. Exposure to such messages, particularly when the accompanying image is compelling, can make it more likely that the image and message is retained in the subconscious memory. If the message plays on an existing bias, even a benign attitude that veterans should be given priority treatment, then the more this bias is confirmed and connected to similar anti-immigration themes, the more it will build support for tougher border policies. Such attitudes can also lead recipients to hold anti-immigrant attitudes and potentially be more accepting of more extreme racist arguments. Put simply, the danger in this and similar cases is that such messages sneak through defences, perhaps when the receiver is emotionally susceptible, not prepared to critically evaluate propaganda, on the commute home from work perhaps. But independent of a lack of concentration, or perhaps because of it, there can be a significant effect for democratic culture.

The work of psychologist Daniel Kahnemann, working with Twersky on work collected in *Thinking Fast, Thinking Slow*, developed the dual process model of thinking. In order to test the extent that people critically reflect, they developed the Cognitive Reflection Test (CRT), in which the most famous question included is the one about the bat and the ball. Their hypothesis is that people who fail to answer CRT questions correctly (usually from a bank of five or seven) are generally unlikely to utilise their capacity for critical thinking. In suggesting that these people, who form the majority, traverse the world relying on what they call system-one thinking, they argue that decisions are often made using erroneous assumptions and partial information. One experiment Kahnemann cites as evidence finds a strong correlation between assessments of a political candidate's competence, based purely on a picture, and electoral success. Alexander Todorov and colleagues (2009) showed graduate students pictures of candidates for as little as one tenth of a second and ask them to rate each against certain attributes. Comparing their rating with actual results showed a significant correlation in 70% or the elections. In a follow up experiment, Lenz and Lawson (2011) found that such judgments were made most often by those with low levels of political knowledge and who were heavy television viewers. If we consider that these same people may constitute society's have-nots, consider the impact on these people, who also proved most likely to vote for Brexit, of the Daily Mail front page article which showed an image of a group of illegal immigrants from Iraq emerging from the back of a lorry at a British port with accompanying headline "We're from Europe, let us in".The power of the simple heuristic not only confirmed beliefs about the concerns of open-door migration from Europe but also showed people who were Muslims entering the country, all popular tropes of the Brexit campaign and concerns within have-not communities in the UK. A combination of system-one thinking and confirmation bias in this case may have had high potential persuasive power.

## GOING BEYOND DUAL PROCESSES

While the neat comparison between the use of system-one thinking (relying on quick, gut responses to stimuli) and system-two thinking (careful and logical critical evaluation) is compelling and minimalist, arguably it is too simple to be universally true. Independent of levels of intelligence, education or knowledge, anyone can succumb to system-one thinking. Lack of interest, lack of time, inability to concentrate and insufficient knowledge are all factors that might reduce the likelihood of system two information processing. One might also suggest that there may be a scale with full system one at one pole and full system two on the opposite. Perhaps a more nuanced approach can be developed by combining the link between thinking and decision making offered by Kahnemann and Twersky with theories of attitude change. Richard E. Petty and John T. Cacioppo (2012) developed the elaboration likelihood model to demonstrate the difference between the subconscious assimilation of simple associations and the formation of informed attitudes. The peripheral route to attitude change involves the semi-subconscious absorption of simple heuristics (images, slogans and associations) on which attitudes can be based. If one views a consistent diet of headlines which link the words Muslims and terrorist, or immigrants and criminal, these associations underpin negative attitudes towards these groups. Similarly, seeing a picture of a politician alongside the word hope may build a positive perception of that candidate. In the first case, the individual may not consider the math: what proportion of Muslims are terrorists and what proportion of immigrants commit crime. In the latter case the individual does not consider what hope means and whether their hopes will be fulfilled by the election of that politician. But these associations, it is argued, as with system-one thinking, can lead to attitude formation and actively supporting a campaign.

The likelihood to elaborate is facilitated by having the motivation and ability, unconstrained by lack of knowledge, time or interest. The central route to attitude change involves the careful consideration of new information, its comparison to the knowledge one possesses and the individual's extant attitudes. Within this process, as with system-two thinking, an individual may remain undecided until they have further data. But the result, both strands of research demonstrate, is an informed attitude that in turn underpins informed decision making. What is particularly useful about the elaboration likelihood model, in contrast to the dual thinking model which appears to use the CRT to make assumptions about the cognitive ability of the individual, is that we are given insights into the conditions which govern critical thinking. When we consider motivations (interest and perceived salience) and ability (time and knowledge) one can imagine four continuums. An election, for example, may stimulate some degree of interest but high perceived salience; knowledge of the contenders may be partial but time limited. Under these conditions one may imagine across the life cycle of a campaign differential levels of elaboration. One may absorb cues from posters or social media adverts uncritically on the commute, in the evening think a little harder during news of the main contenders positions, concentrate at points during a televised debate and then revert to absorbing a few more cues from social media while sipping cocoa before bed. If this makes sense when reflecting on your own behaviour, then it is simple to imagine that every citizen might, on average, sit across a spectrum of elaboration likelihood. Furthermore, any individual may sit at different points on that spectrum in relation to politics during a campaign and indeed generally during one's lifetime.

## THE SUBCONSCIOUS AND THE SCHEMA

The challenge is then to imagine what drives decision making, what information do people retain and from where and what influence does this information have. It is useful to imagine the memory as a filing system made up of an infinite number of folders, just like the folder one might create on the desktop of a computer. At election time, one may have a folder marked with the name of a candidate or party. Within that, there will be general information and subfolders, some for policies, for values or for specific items of personal relevance. There may also be sub-subfolders, each with general and specific information stored away. Not every person's memory will have the same folders, some will have a folder for environment others may not. Also, not everyone's folders will contain the same information or the same quality or quantity of detail.

Schema theory, as outlined here, allows us to thus understand how individuals collect and file data, which allow us to more easily navigate our world. The information that allows us to recognise a table and a politician who might be lying is different obviously, but the process is the same. But back to the folders. Inside each folder may be some well-defined information, the result of critical consideration driven by high motivation and ability. Alongside this, in the same folder, a subfolder or even the master folder, there will be simplistic, meaningless or inaccurate heuristics (Grumpy Cat says vote Democrat, a headline linking immigration rates to crime, a political candidate pictured with a popular actor, a comparison of a medical face mask to a dog's muzzle). Combining these bits of information and sorting them by relevance, by frequency and by credibility aids the formation of an attitude. The resulting attitudes can range from very weak to very strong, depending on the quality and quantity of information held. Holistically though, what one may gain from this is a picture of how information processing contributes to attitudes and so shapes behaviour. The question is to what extent are schemas relating to candidates, parties or policy areas made up mainly of heuristics and the origins of that material. This leads us to the challenge for democracy: the extent that decision making might be driven by system-one, peripheral processing of information based on heuristics and confirmation bias.

## HEURISTICS AND BIASES: THE MANIPULATED CITIZEN

Heuristics are mental shortcuts that are utilised to help reach a workable answer to a complex question. Some argue that religion provides some of the most powerful heuristics possible. Why is the world as it is? Because our god wills it to be. There is no need to delve into social or natural science; equally there is no way to counter such a response. However, most decisions are not driven by divine intervention. Imagine you are planning to buy a new car. There are literally hundreds of models of automobiles available; the choice is complex. Firstly, we discount those outside of our price range, possibly including finance limits. Next, we might consider the functionality, is it a family car, a status symbol, best for a cheap local commute or for frequent long-distance drives. Endorsements from friends may help identify a narrower set of options. Then you visit a dealership, the final factor is the feeling on seeing the car and sitting in it. The cost aspect can involve simple comparison, exploration of options and some degree of deliberation, not exactly second order but more in-depth than first-order peripheral processing. The views of others can lead to hot cognition, moments of intense mental stimulation running alongside second-order central route information processing. The final phase will be purely emotional. Feelings are powerful heuristics in themselves that can lead to hot but focused thinking. So, for this important decision, the file may contain price information, promotional communication from car brands, write-ups and reviews in magazines, comments and suggestions from friends and the feelings experienced. Much of the content will be heuristics, small aspects of this information that is deemed most important and relevant.

Bias can creep into the organisation of information in a schema. Firstly, we may prioritise feeling over more logical information. Secondly, certain images may stand out, because they capture the image we want to have or represent the specific function we are seeking. Thirdly we may rely on the endorsement of the source we feel is the most credible, which can be the friend we most want to emulate or impress as opposed to the one with the most expertise. While feelings automatically bias our decision making, the other heuristics are purely external stimuli that may be given greater credence than they are worth. However, these sorts of heuristics, prioritised according to individual biases, may commonly be used to make judgments when the choice is complex.

If we extend the thinking to politics, one can hypothesise that a narrower group of heuristics and more biased process for selection could be employed. Some of the reasons given for supporting Brexit included the globalisation of the UK high street and the preponderance of uniformity from town to town; the notion of being swamped by migrant workers with the favourite heuristic being foreign food shops; the imposition of rules, for example governing health and safety, with the reference point being newspaper headlines rather than recognising that these are the product of demands from insurance companies; or the loss of sovereignty referencing singular standout stories of judgments from the European Court of Justice which is actually independent of the EU (see Lilleker & Liefbroer, 2018). Each of these examples may hide a plethora of pieces of information, however, they evidence a reliance on heuristics to reinforce a perspective and each highlights a bias towards the EU as a negative force on the UK in some way or another. Data which suggests that heuristics and bias impact election outcomes, such as that detailed previously, offer an indication that voters are gamblers. Voters assess the probability that they are right and privilege their assessment over ensuring they are certain they have sufficient evidence to support their decision.

This phenomenon leads van Zoonen (2012) to talk of i-pistemology replacing epistemology. Epistemology is the science of knowledge, what quality and quantity of data is required in order to have certainty at one time and over time. I-pistemology suggests that beliefs are prioritised and, building on the discussion of confirmation bias, if a decision is consistent with existing beliefs and behavioural patterns it is more likely to be given credence. The problem is that beliefs may be based on sub-optimal evidence, in fact, beliefs are defined as being difficult or impossible to prove incontrovertibly. Heuristics, in the form of images and video, can offer impressions of political candidates, parties or institutions which can be wholly false. Those who use a narrow diet of media may be exposed to positive images of one candidate which are countered elsewhere but due to reliance on a narrow range of information sources and a homogenous social network such information may never be seen. Low motivation leads to a reliance on those images and a flawed voter decision.

Even a person who pays some attention, or even constant partial attention, to an election campaign can be susceptible to manipulation from carefully crafted heuristics. A debate between leaders can be lacklustre with few moments that inspire emotional or cognitive engagement. Yet one image can have resonance, causing a strong emotional reaction, leading to central processing of the argument and an attitudinal impact. However, paying partial attention does not allow for critical examination of an argument in full, and hence the resultant reasoning is based on partial but resonant information or indeed quick assessments.

Quick assessments can be particularly problematic when we consider performance as a heuristic. The visual dimension of a performance, or particular images, can lead to a lasting impression: does a political candidate show competence, likeability, etc. (on the power of visuals in politics see Veneti et al., 2019)? One aspect of performance is a rhetoric of authenticity, as Michael Saward puts it "I can speak for or represent these marginalised interests because no one is paying me to do so, because I have no other axe to grind as all elected officials do, because I am the real thing, authentic" (Saward, 2005, p. 193). Feminist scholar Shirin Rai (2015) talks of a variety of visual heuristics which contribute to authenticity. Firstly, authenticity pertains to the body, how someone looks and is dressed offers information about their social status and the extent they fit their role and connect to their audience. Secondly, Rai talks of the place, space and stage they inhabit, or are seen to inhabit; they might always be seen among certain elite groups or among a diverse range of ordinary people or they might be seen mostly within the confines of a parliament or at a rally. Thirdly, there is the verbal performative aspects, what they say, the words they use and the tone and inflection of voice. Finally, she discusses their performative labour, what they do to evidence their position vis-à-vis wider society. Each of these can be manufactured to create a composite image of the individual. But in themselves, each is a value-laden cue.

If a politician dresses as any man or woman in the street might dress, is pictured among politicians and diverse groups of citizens, uses the language and rhetoric of ordinary citizens and is known to have had 'normal' jobs, not just working within political parties, they may be viewed as authentic, in-touch and so connected to the wider community. In contrast, a politician wearing designer suits, who roams the world's political stage, uses an elite linguistic style and appears comfortable making deals with national leaders might be seen as embedded in a system and less 'in-touch'. Yet, in either case, the judgement regarding who might be the better national leader is which is most appealing to the individual.

Hence, authenticity has been compared by Norwegian political communication scholar Gunn Enli with beauty: it is a matter of personal taste and perspective. Individuals have their own ideas of what constitutes beauty in architecture, art and nature. One person's idea of beauty may be seen as bland or even ugly by someone else. Authenticity is similar. The reason is because the majority cannot tell whether the politician's performance is authentic or the performance of authenticity. Good actors are good because they are able to make an audience believe in the characters they play. A character can be one we can like, fear for, hate, fear, empathise with and perhaps all of these; the basis for this belief is how the actor conveys how the character feels. Audiences read the emotions portrayed and react. Few candidates who would be a national leader are actors, although Reagan, Schwarzenegger or Zelensky are exceptions, none of these are renowned for their range or skill for character portrayal. Hence, perhaps, they are judged on their ability to perform as a human as opposed to an expert in character portrayal. The distinction here is that the expectation is that what is seen is what is real, whereas an actor is expected to be non-existent and the character is foregrounded.

Authenticity, in theory at least, is something all politicians' performances should contain. The innateness of authenticity in the performances of politicians has however been brought into question over the past decades. Discussions of the practices of impression and image management within the media, alongside the issues relating to political spin and propaganda, has exposed the roles of speechwriters, fashion advisers, dressers and public relations advisors in the background, all of which question the authenticity of the performance. The greater awareness of the processes that provide the foundations for a performance leads to more sceptical and potentially critical audiences. Perhaps because of this scepticism, or exacerbating it, are the judgment values audience members impose on politicians. If emotions are not conveyed, in the case of Germany's Chancellor Angela Merkel or the UK's 2008–10 prime minister Gordon Brown, the inference is they lack empathy and feelings. Similarly, female politicians can suffer both from displaying strength as well as emotion, UK prime minister (2016–19) Theresa May was criticised for crying but also for 'not crying' during a short period of time. Hence many politicians are judged either as lacking authenticity or either being insufficiently or overly emotional.

The previous examples suggest that a uniform view emerges of any given actor, though in some cases it can be true that a candidate can perform so well they unite the majority behind them, or so badly the majority reject them. However, some political actors can be seen as polarising characters, encouraging love and hate from differing societal sections. Pablo Iglesias, Leader of Spanish leftist Podemos party, is seen by some of his supporters as being driven by values he holds and speaking for them; his political enemies accuse him of subterfuge and obfuscation. Similar themes emerge around US President (2016–21) Donald Trump and UK prime minister (2019–) Boris Johnson. This phenomenon returns us to our discussion of confirmation bias in chapter two. While perceptions of beauty may be a matter of taste, perceptions of authenticity in politics may be driven by political allegiance. Trump is viewed as the authentic voice of the rust-belt residents of middle America, the voice of their discontent and exclusion. Opponents argue he is devious, uses dog whistle politics to appeal to Americans with racist and misogynistic tendencies and uses communication to attract votes through tropes that divide rather than unite. Hence, in such circumstances, how close a voter feels to that candidate and the positions they espouse can be crucial.

## PROXIMITY: HOW SIMILARITY, CLOSENESS AND RELEVANCE CAN LEAD TO HOT COGNITION

Within the realm of social psychology, there are two complementary approaches that explain our judgments and calculations when engaging with the message of a politician: *proximity* and *valence*. As in the previous section, we defined proximity as how close we feel a politician to be to ourselves. There are two types of proximity that affect our thinking process, namely physical and emotional. The physical proximity principle suggests that people have the tendency to form interpersonal relations with individuals who they are familiar with and who are similar to them in aspects that are important for that individual's identity. Emotional proximity, on the other hand, relates to a strong attraction due to sharing similar values and perspectives.

The founder of this approach, Leon Festinger (1954), developed physical proximity out of research on students living in dormitory rooms. They found that the more another student was encountered, the stronger the bond; sharing a room proved strongest, then a corridor, then a building. The bond for the other student in turn induces them to gravitate towards his/her message, for example during student elections. In politics, the extent to which citizens are exposed to a candidate and their message will also influence perceptions. Exposure to a candidate through mass or social media channels enhances positive feelings. It seems that the more someone is seen, the more likely they are liked (Perloff, 2013). On the one hand, the proximity approach assists us in understanding the strategies of authoritarian leaders such as the Syrian dictator Hafiz Al Assad and his son, Bashar, who bedecked the walls of buildings, the windows of taxi cabs and even the doors of restaurants with their images. This type of exposure might not always lead to feelings of liking, and we know that not every Syrian likes the Assad family, but all citizens were regularly reminded of the authority of these leaders (Weeden, 1998, p. 54). In democracies, however, for politicians such as Donald Trump, Boris Johnson, Vladimir Zelensky and others who have enjoyed a high media profile for a number of years, proximity may explain why at least some voters have a strong attachment to them.

Self (1996) argues that proximity is not simply about the individual. Repetition can foster familiarity with a message and enhance its credibility. Even if the repeated message is false, if it is memorable and repeated it can be retained and impact voter attitudes. Campaign slogans are particularly important for this form of proximity. For example, during the 2019 UK general election, the slogan "Get Brexit done" was repeated on every billboard, pamphlet and doorstep and on every media appearance by leader Boris Johnson. The Conservative Party even created a lo-fi hip hop song featuring the slogan. "Get Brexit done" was a deliberate oversimplification, which Johnson knew, as even though Britain would legally be out of the EU by 31 January 2020, the trade negotiations with the bloc would continue thereafter. Yet, by repeating the same message over and over, Johnson managed create a strong association with the idea that he would solve the issue that had proven intractable for the previous three years. Many commentators argue this delivered Johnson a decisive victory. Similar tactics have been used to encourage compliance with measures to limit the spread of Covid-19. French citizens were asked to adopt a wartime mentality to bring the nation together and Iraqis to be health 'jihadis'. Elsewhere, variations on the theme of 'Stay Home; Save Lives' were employed. The American cognitive linguist Lakoff (2004) termed this the "repeat and remind" tactic. The repetition of a slogan over and over again ensures it penetrates the audience's consciousness and leads to behavioural compliance, a well-established tactic used in advertising and public relations.

Aside from familiarity with a source or message, emotional connectedness and empathy for someone are also determinants of proximity. Social psychology scholars Hodges and Myers (2007) argue emotional closeness has three dimensions: sharing emotions with or feeling empathy with an individual are the first two. The third and most powerful is a combination of the two. They argue that the strongest feelings of proximity are when citizens sense that others share the same problems as they do and understand their everyday experiences. A good example of both the physical and emotional proximity effects can be found during the 2011 Egyptian protests. Egyptian activists knew people needed a good reason to sacrifice their time and potentially risk their lives by joining anti-Mubarak protests (Tarrow, 2011, p. ii). Thus, to mobilise poorer groups in Egyptian society, the activists needed to show empathy with their problems. Egyptian protesters divided into small groups based on their social and cultural backgrounds. Each of these would then go to the areas with which they identified. Here, they could talk directly about the common grievances of citizens across Egypt. The mobilisation campaign enjoyed overwhelming success, with protests attracting a wide cross-section of Egyptian society (Ozgul, 2019).

Thus, proximity covers simple familiarity as well as strategic and rhetorical devices for indicating closeness. All aspects are argued to help voters with lower resources to cognitively measure the choices on offer. Whiteley et al. (2013) explains, voters first assess politicians' positions on one or more ideological or policy dimensions (such as tax cuts or medical services). They ask, "is this person close to me on the issues that matter to me?" and "will they make decisions

I would agree with?". To maximise their utilities, they then vote for the party that is closest to them in the space defined by these dimensions. However, proximity may not be sufficient, the message also has to resonate with the audience.

## VALENCE THEORY

What proximity theories do not account for is that many voters do not have in-depth knowledge of the policy positions and ideologies of political candidates. For instance, during the 2016 American election, a Pew research survey of 1,000 US citizens showed that "only about half of voters (48%) say they know 'a lot' about where Clinton stands on important issues, while even fewer (41%) say this about Trump". This problem is further compounded by the fact that populist political candidates tend to hold few sincere policy beliefs. Voters can also find it challenging to see a clear link between espoused positions and underlying values. Tankersley (2016) argues that Donald Trump's platform, for instance, consisted mainly of 'non-attitudes'. Trump could advocate single-payer health care in one interview and oppose it in another. Hilary Clinton, on the other hand, who lost the 2016 presidential election against Trump, had a more coherent stand, with a clear desire for higher taxes, more redistribution and more regulation. In 2020, the choices became more simplistic. Biden voters saw him as more likely to tackle Covid-19, address issues of racial inequality and bring the country together. Trump voters simply wanted the economy to be the priority, they felt the pandemic should not be prioritised and racial inequality to them lacked valence.

Valence theory explains this phenomenon by asserting that cues play an important role in the political decision-making process. Perceptions of which candidate or party appears the best to deal with the issues we care about may have greater influence than a rounded evaluation of a political programme. Perceived competence is one such cue. In the 2020 US election, Biden was ahead in perceptions of competence for those concerned about the pandemic. But for many white working class who believed they 'deserve better', Trump was deemed to have the competence to deliver them a more secure future (Henley, 2016). By addressing the white working class's concerns in his speeches, Trump's promises resonated and were valent, hence they voted for him to restore "what they believe is their rightful place in the national pecking order" (Lamont et al., 2017). His promises during the 2016 and 2020 campaigns had greater valence among the white 'have-nots' in US society.

Research into how people judge the credibility of a candidate, found that aside from perceived competence, audiences make assessments of character, in particular, composure, dynamism and sociability (Burgoon et al., 2000). Obama's smile, for instance, was often seen as warm and inviting. Romney, on the other hand, was conceived as being strained and slightly distant (Saad, 2012). The former was thus more sociable. Character perceptions can also draw on prejudices and stereotypes. O'Brien explored voter perceptions of female party leaders. Her research discovered that female leaders were viewed as more moderate and less extreme than their male counterparts, despite some female leaders in reality being slightly more extreme (O'Brien, 2019). Cultural stereotypes of females induced the perception of them being less threatening, which is argued to explain the steady rise in the number of female-led political parties in different parts of the world, such as in Germany, Denmark, New Zealand and, until recently, the UK and France, with French voters seeing the Front National under Marine le Pen as more mainstream than when it was led by her father.

Secondly, citizens could make decisions by comparing party performance on the most important problems facing the country: valence issues. Common valence issues are having a strong economy with a low level of unemployment, a secure state, a good health care system etc. While citizens often disagree as to who can best provide these (Whiteley et al., 2013), some parties tend to own certain issues. A recent YouGov survey showed that, despite the popularity of the Labour Party's policies in the UK, the party was not perceived as being competent to deliver a good economy by 57% of the UK electorate in 2019. The perception existed that "the country will go into economic recession within a couple of years if Labour win the election". Two factors explain this. Firstly, the Conservative Party had frequently stated that the Labour Party was responsible for the 2008 recession, not the global economic crisis (Chivers, 2015). Secondly, centre-right parties like the conservatives tend to be viewed as having higher levels of economic competence naturally (for a debate on this, see Bélanger & Nadeau, 2015).

This highlights the importance of political parties appearing competent across a vast range of issues. This is because a nation's valence issues can change over time due to scarcity or socialisation. The things we most lack have the highest salience (importance), governed by the context in which we grow up. For example, democracy may be more valued by someone socialised under totalitarianism. Job security may be more valued by someone growing up in a deprived area. If the salient issue is under threat, those who value it most are likely to have the strongest emotional reaction (Inglehart, 1997). For example, while the Egyptians were more concerned about poverty and the economy before 2011, following the 2011 protests, the common issue that united Egyptian citizens was stability (Gamal & Inwood, 2016). The issue fiercely divided Egyptian society into two segments: one believed the Sisi government was the only option for bringing stability and the other feeling that Sisi was the cause of current instability. Hence, it is important that the political parties adapt their discourses and images according to the socio- economic, political conditions of their era.

Finally, party identification can also serve as a cue which activates latent partisan biases in the minds of citizens. Consequently, voters are more interested in messages emanating from the party they identify with. Yet, according to valence theorists, party identification is not a definite predictor of voting behaviour. Attitudes towards a party can change according to its recent performance and the perceived character and competence of its leader. This suggests there is no fixed partisan attachment. Rather, voters may change their allegiances due to feelings of proximity and the valence of communication: for example, the working-class Labour supporters who chose to cast their votes for Johnson in the 2019 UK election in order to 'Get Brexit Done'. This represents a perfect example where a leader's familiarity, perceived empathy with the cause of the Brexit-voting have-nots and message salience shows how proximity and valence drove voter choices.

## POLITICAL JUDGMENTS

Image factors are arguably even more important in the digital age, where the self 'mediatisation' shapes perceptions. A leadership candidate is expected to show authenticity and empathy, ordinariness as well as an extraordinary character, elements that feature at the heart of the intangible qualities that constitute charisma (Marshall & Henderson, 2016). Hence, leaders attempt to find ways to directly communicate an image to the electorate, communication that offers cues as to the character of the real person behind the politician. Former UK prime minister, David Cameron, created a video weblog (Web-Cameron) to create emotional connection with his audience. Cameron regularly invited his audience into his kitchen over this weblog, where he answered their questions while undertaking mundane chores. Hardman (2015) claims that the vlog permitted Cameron to perform ordinariness and empathy, focusing on building a persona. The performed persona was human and approachable, which put the audience at ease with him. Non-partisan voters found him to be more likeable, a key segment required for Cameron's conservatives to emerge as the party with most MPs in the 2010 election. The more personal and emotional relationship developed led to higher levels of trust that Cameron would empathise with voter needs and demands. US president Trump has developed an authentic persona through his use of Twitter, a performance that displays ordinariness while representing the voice of angry white America. Hence, judgements may be more easily manipulated in the digital age. Social judgment theory explained how leaders can increase the acceptance of their messages in the digital age. When voters develop strong positive attitudes towards an individual leader, they are more likely to support their program, hence simple image cues that engender high proximity can be a strong determinant of voter choices.

Brenda Cooper's (1998) research helps us to understand how attitudes influence reception of a message. She analysed white and black students' reactions to Spike Lee's movie, "*Do the Right Thing*". The movie is a disturbing and controversial portrait of relationships amongst black, white and Hispanic individuals in New York City. Sal, one of the main characters in the film, is an Italian American. He owns a pizzeria that is decorated with the photos of Italian Americans. The paradox is that Sal's customers are mostly African American. One day, two black-Hispanic customers protest the absence of photos of African American people on his pizzeria's walls. Their protest involves playing their music loudly and when they refuse to lower the volume of their radio, Sal smashes it with a baseball bat, and calls them 'niggers', instigating a brawl. The police arrive and while restraining one of the black-Hispanic protesters a white police officer kills him. After showing the movie, Cooper asked students to describe their reactions to the movie. In accordance with social judgment theory, the perceptions of white students differed considerably from those of black students. The theme of police brutality was virtually ignored by white students and they also did not consider Sal's refusal to put photos of famous African American people on his pizzeria's "wall of fame" to be racist. Some thought that the film created controversy amongst the spectators because of Lee's unfair depictions of whites as racist. On the other hand, African American students defined Sal's actions and his relationship with his black customers as "racist, exploitative, and more importantly, as representative of the larger issues of black oppression in American society".

Hence, unlike the white American students, the African American students considered the movie from a wider perspective. The movie tapped into an issue they found salient, black discrimination in American society, and could not interpret Sal's actions outside to the wider context. The images in the movie evoked several schemas: black resistance to oppression and repression by white people. They also identified with the portrayed characters and found the racism salient as it resonated with their personal life experiences and cultural sub-jectivities (Cooper, 1998).

Persuasion theorists remind us that a message receiver can take three different types of positions towards an issue. The first is the latitude of acceptance. On an attitude scale, this position is the most acceptable to a person on a given topic. Second is the latitude of rejec-tion, where the position is received negatively. Finally, there is the lat-itude of non-commitment, where the receiver is neutral towards the position of the communicator (Kunczik, 2008). Cooper's research showed that oppression towards black people was a hot button issue for the African American students and that they were predisposed to reject alternative perspectives. White American students, on the other hand, who identified more with Sal, did not find the portrayal of him by Lee, who is black himself, relevant to reality. The messages from Lee about ongoing racism in America fell into their latitude of rejec-tion. The study shows that an American political candidate who wants to persuade the different groups in the US must be careful while framing hot button issues such as this. Whether the receivers have weak or strong attitudes towards an issue, the first task of a political candidate is to know their position and then to make sure that his/her arguments tap into the existing values, beliefs and attitudes of the different receivers so that it is assimilated into their schema.

A good example of this strategy was employed by a group of young supporters of the UK's 'Leave the EU' campaign who call themselves 'BeLeave' campaigners. During the referendum, BeLeave campaign-ers tried to convince migrants from the Commonwealth with British passports to vote Leave via a Facebook page. The campaigners knew that this segment of society valued immigration and so could not use the broad anti-immigration messages common to the Leave cam-paign, as these would be automatically rejected. Instead, they argued that what Leavers actually wanted was equal rights for all immigrants. The argument was that by being in the EU, the UK had to privi-lege migrants from the EU over Commonwealth citizens. The dis-course tapped into broad normative values of how democracy should operate. As social judgment theory asserts, for the argument to be retained, it is essential that we frame it in as relevant a way as possible. The BeLeave campaign thus chimed with values as well as more selfish motivations of migrants who wished to have family join them in the UK, which the current quota system prevented.

Delivering such tailored messages was challenging in the age of mass media. However social media trace data not only records demographic details, but also data on the content that each user likes and shares. Campaigners can access this data and produce communication with maximum valence and salience. During the 2016 US presidential election, for instance, messages were targeted at different groups with positive messages about Donald Trump's bid for the presidency. For example, while some messages promoted African American rights groups, including Black Lives Matter, others portrayed the same group as a political threat to the US citizens and it was claimed that these messages were the result of external interference (Entous, 2017). Insider accounts of the operations of Cambridge Analytica suggest that social media platforms were used to manipulate US voters, as well as voters in the UK and Nigeria (see Wylie, 2019).

Such tactics can increase the familiarity of certain messages and convince voters of positions which are wholly inaccurate. For example, 18% of Americans polled by Pew Research in 2010 believed that then US president Barack Obama was a Muslim born outside of the US. Individuals can also build perceptions of the character and persona, all of which increases feelings of proximity among their audiences. Through addressing widely held concerns, they can increase their valence, and if combined with high proximity and positive character attributes, this can prove to be a winning formula. Such tactics can be employed by any politician, from the mainstream Cameron to the populist Trump. If voters subsequently feel they have been misled, this can have a deleterious impact for democratic engagement. With data traces constituting important means for manipulating voter choices, there may be greater opportunities for voters to be misled and trust in democratic processes and institutions to be damaged. Any politician with the right strategy and resources can manufacture higher proximity and valence, hence Trump, who as a businessman decried worker's rights (Laughland & Ryan, 2016), was able to win the votes of white working-class Americans.

## REFERENCES

Bélanger, É., & Nadeau, R. (2015). Issue ownership of the economy: Cross-time effects on vote choice. *West European Politics*, 38(4), 909–932. https://doi.org/10.1080/01402382.2015.1039373

Burgoon, J. K., Bonito, J. A., Bengtsson, B., Cederberg, C., Lundeberg, M., & Allspach, L. (2000). Interactivity in human – computer interaction: A study of credibility, understanding, and influence. *Computers in Human Behavior*, 16(6), 553–574. https://doi.org/10.1016/S0747-5632(00)00029-7

Chivers, D. (2015, May 5). Fact check: Did labour overspend and leave a deficit that was out of control. *The Conversation*. http://theconversation.com/fact-check-did-labour-overspend-and-leave-a-deficit-that-was-out-of-control-41118

Cooper, B. (1998). "The White-Black fault line": Relevancy of race and racism in spectators' experiences of Spike Lee's do the right thing. *Howard Journal of Communication*, 9(3), 205–228. https://doi.org/10.1080/106461798246998

Entous, A. (2017, September 25). Russian operatives used Facebook ads to exploit America's racial and religious divisions. *The Washington Post*. www.washingtonpost.com/business/technology/russian-operatives-used-facebook-ads-to-exploit-divisions-over-black-political-activism-and-muslims/2017/09/25/4a011242-a21b-11e7-ade1-76d061d56efa_story.html

Festinger, L. (1954). A theory of social comparison processes. *Human Relations*, 7(2), 117–140. https://doi.org/10.1177/001872675400700202

Gamal, R., & Inwood, J. (2016, January 25). Egypt's revolution five-year anniversary sees hashtag battle. BBC. www.bbc.co.uk/news/av/world-middle-east-35384770/egypt-s-revolution-five-year-anniversary-sees-hashtag-battle

Gigerenzer, G. (2008). Why heuristics work. *Perspectives on Psychological Science*, 3(1), 20–29. https://doi.org/10.1111/j.1745-6916.2008.00058.x

Hardman, I. (2015, March 17). Cameron's controlled media strategy keeps voters in the kitchen. *The Spectator*. https://blogs.spectator.co.uk/2015/03/camerons-controlled-media-strategy-keeps-voters-in-the-kitchen/

Henley, J. (2016, November 9). White and wealthy voters gave victory to Donald Trump, exit polls show. *The Guardian*. www.theguardian.com/us-news/2016/nov/09/white-voters-victory-donald-trump-exit-polls

Hodges, S. D., & Myers, M. W. (2007). Empathy. In R. F. Baumeister & K. D. Vohs (Eds.), *Encyclopedia of social psychology* (pp. 296–298). Sage.

Kunczik, M. (2008). Latitude of acceptance. In W. Donsbach (Ed.), *The concise encyclopedia of communication* (pp. 326–327). Wiley Blackwell. https://doi.org/10.1002/9781405186407.wbiecl011

Lakoff, G. (2004). *Don't think of an elephant: Progressive values and the framing wars – a progressive guide to action*. Chelsea Green Publishing.

Lamont, M., Park, B. Y., & Ayala-Hurtado, E. (2017). Trump's electoral speeches and his appeal to the American white working class. *British Journal of Sociology*, 68(S1), 153–180.

Laughland, O., & Ryan, M. (2016, May 2). Workers fight for dignity in Trump's Las Vegas hotel: "You don't talk to the boss". *The Guardian*. www.theguardian.com/us-news/2016/may/02/donald-trump-workers-hotel-international-las-vegas

Lenz, G. S., & Lawson, C. (2011). Looking the part: Television leads less informed citizens to vote based on candidates' appearance. *American Journal of Political Science*, 55(3), 574–589. https://doi.org/10.1111/j.1540-5907.2011.00511.x

Lilleker, D. G., & Liefbroer, M. (2018). "Searching for something to believe in": Voter uncertainty in a post-truth environment. *International Journal of Media & Cultural Politics*, 14(3), 351–366. https://doi.org/10.1386/macp.14.3.351_1

Marshall, P. D., & Henderson, N. (2016). Political persona 2016 – an introduction. *Persona Studies*, 2(2), 1–18. https://doi.org/10.21153/ps2016vol2no2art628

O'Brien, D. Z. (2019, November 1). Citizens (mistakenly) perceive female-led political parties as more moderate. *LSE British Politics and Policy*. https://blogs.lse.ac.uk/politicsandpolicy/perceptions-of-female-led-parties/

Ozgul, B. A. (2019). *Leading protests in the digital age: Youth activism in Egypt and Syria*. Palgrave Macmillan. https://doi.org/10.1007/978-3-030-25450-6

Pew. (2016). Ahead of debates, many voters don't know much about where Trump, Clinton stand on major issues. https://www.pewresearch.

org/fact-tank/2016/09/23/ahead-of-debates-many-voters-dont-know-much-about-where-trump-clinton-stand-on-major-issues/

Rai, S. M. (2015). Political performance: A framework for analysing democratic politics. *Political Studies*, 63(5), 1179–1197. https://doi.org/10.1111/1467-9248.12154

Saad, G. (2012, September 30). How do people choose their political leaders? *Psychology Today*. www.psychologytoday.com/us/blog/homo-consumericus/201209/how-do-people-choose-their-political-leaders?amp

Saward, M. (2005). Governance and the transformation of political representation. In J. Newman (Ed.), *Remaking governance: Peoples, politics and the public sphere* (pp. 179–196). Policy Press.

Self, C. S. (1996). Credibility. In M. B. Salwen & D. W. Stacks (Eds.), *An integrated approach to communication theory and research* (Chapter 28). Erlbaum.

Smith, M. (2019). Labour economic policies are popular, so why aren't Labour? https://yougov.co.uk/topics/politics/articles-reports/2019/11/12/labour-economic-policies-are-popular-so-why-arent-

Tankersley, J. (2016, January 11). Hillary Clinton wants the rich to pay higher taxes: Here's how high. *The Washington Post*. www.washingtonpost.com/news/wonk/wp/2016/01/11/hillary-clinton-wants-the-rich-to-pay-higher-taxes-heres-how-high/

Tarrow, S. (2011). *Power in movement*. Cambridge University Press.

Todorov, A., Pakrashi, M., & Oosterhof, N. N. (2009). Evaluating faces on trustworthiness after minimal time exposure. *Social Cognition*, 27(6), 813–833. https://doi.org/10.1521/soco.2009.27.6.813

Van Zoonen, L. (2012). I-pistemology: Changing truth claims in popular and political culture. *European Journal of Communication*, 27(1), 56–67. https://doi.org/10.1177/0267323112438808

Weeden, L. (1998). Acting "as if": Symbolic politics and social control in Syria. *Comparative Studies in Society and History*, 40(3), 503–523. https://doi.org/10.1017/S0010417598001388

Whiteley, P., Clarke, H. D., Sanders, D., & Stewart, M. C. (2013). *Affluence, austerity and electoral change in Britain*. Cambridge University Press. https://doi.org/10.1017/CBO9781139162517

Wylie, C. (2019). *Mindf*ck: Inside Cambridge analytica's plot to break the world*. Profile Books.

## FURTHER READING

Enli, G. (2015). *Mediated authenticity: How the media constructs reality.* Peter Lang.

Inglehart, R. (1997). *Modernization and postmodernization: Cultural, economic and political change in 43 societies.* Princeton University Press.

Kahneman, D., & Egan, P. (2011). *Thinking, fast and slow.* New York: Random House Audio.

Perloff, R. M. (2013). *The dynamics of political communication: Media and politics in a digital age.* Routledge.

Petty, R. E., & Cacioppo, J. T. (2012). *Communication and persuasion: Central and peripheral routes to attitude change.* Springer. https://doi.org/10.1007/978-1-4612-4964-1

Veneti, A., Jackson, D., & Lilleker, D. G. (Eds.). (2019). *Visual political communication.* Palgrave Macmillan. https://doi.org/10.1007/978-3-030-18729-3

# 4

---

# POLITICAL PARTICIPATION

## DEMOCRATIC CITIZENSHIP

Being a citizen comes with a set of rights. Constitutions or the rule of law protect personal integrity, freedom of speech, religious liberty, freedom of thought and the right to property. Citizens are also given protections, by laws and by welfare programs. Politically a citizen has the right to vote in elections and have equal opportunity to be elected. But being a citizen also comes with responsibilities. Citizenship is frequently related to being informed and taking an active role in social and civic culture, hence, to be a citizen is to be a participant in democratic life. Classical definitions of political participation focus on voting, standing for election or attempting to influence organisations and individuals with political power. These normally involve some form of collective action, even if the action, such as voting or signing a petition, is an individual act. More recently, participation is understood to encompass a range of behaviours which incorporate the various actions which occur through digital platforms (from email to Twitter and beyond) and the act of protest. While being a citizen involves conforming to the law while performing one's civic responsibilities, in order to be heard, at times one must contravene some laws if the issue being protested is sufficiently important. The citizen makes the decision that their responsibility to act outweighs the constraints of the law. Hence political participation can take a

DOI: 10.4324/9781003021292-4

range of forms, some of which can involve transgression. This chapter explores why people participate and take part in a variety of forms of participation while also considering the flipside and considering why people might eschew their civic responsibilities and reject their role within democratic processes.

## MOTIVATED PARTICIPATION

Whether the action is within or outside the law, in a simple act such as liking or even posting about politics on social media, voting or lobbying a representative, there must be some form of motivational stimuli. It is useful to consider motivations by focusing on the more effortful forms of participation. Perhaps the most effortful and dramatic form of political participation is the protest, one which involves personal risk and can involve stepping outside the boundaries of the rule of law. Yet, protests are a long-established method for influencing public debates, the actions of governments or even bringing about regime change. Anti-austerity protests in Greece in 2010, the Arab spring protests in Syria and Egypt in 2011 and most recently the 2020 Black Lives Matter (BLM) protests provide excellent examples for exploring the possible motivations of protestors. Drawing on Frijda (2004), we propose a continuum approach to understanding participation. We show how four motivational determinants can cause emotional reactions to external stimuli to lead to higher levels of cognitive involvement. According to Frijda (2004), the action performed depends on the context: how acceptable the action is and will it result in an acceptable outcome, the repertoire of actions that are available, the perceived importance of the event and whether there is social support or disapproval – what he refers to as the social eye.

Discussing acceptability, Frijda (2004, p. 163) argues that participation depends on networks of concerns: does participation involve acceptable levels of personal risk and are there systemic risks which could be exacerbated. Personal risk depends very much on perceptions of the state's response. At the beginning of the 2011

Syrian protests, the middle-class was afraid of being arrested and imprisoned. There was also a lack of hope that regime policy would change and low political efficacy; to large swathes of Syrian society protesting was unacceptable (Ozgul, 2019, p. 43). Even when state brutality is not a fear, other outcomes may concern protestors. During the 2009 Greek financial crisis, many worried protests could result in their country's exit from the Eurozone and an even deeper financial crisis (Davou & Demertzis, 2013, p. 99). Hence, the risk of this unintended potential consequence made the action unacceptable. If citizens think an action can have a negative personal impact or worsen a political situation, they are less likely to find an action acceptable unless communication from within a protest movement can overcome this by encouraging citizens to believe their action will lead to a positive outcome.

The second motivational determinant, availability, can increase acceptability. Frijda (2004) argued that the more experience one has with a form of action, the more likely it will be acceptable as part of a repertoire of responses to a problem. The Movement for Black Lives was founded in 2015 on the back of two years of sporadic protesting under the banner of Black Lives Matter (BLM). The long experience of BLM protests, and the impact on public consciousness evidenced during the protests, for example the fact that the "BlackLivesMatter" hashtag was used 1.7 million times on Twitter in 2013 (Leach & Allen, 2017, p. 544), indicated that protests were an available part of the movement's repertoire. There was also a high level of organisational experience of protest to draw upon. However, in nations where freedom of speech is restricted, often there is no experience, and protesting is seen as unavailable. Wael Ghonim, one of the organisers of the 25th January 2011 protests in Egypt, testified that opposing the state was scary at first. In 2010, when the leading opposition figure, ElBaradei, called on Egyptians to boycott parliamentary elections and sign a petition, it took Ghonim two days to decide to join this action. Yet, seeing the support for the petition turned Ghonim's fear into excitement (Ghonim, 2012, p. 46). Protest became an available form of action as there was significant support for change and so the possibility of having an impact. Yet still when the 2011 Egyptian and Syrian protests started, those with low levels of experience felt less able to protest. But their personal fears were allayed by those with experience, providing a support network for protestors. Egyptian activists prepared themselves for big clashes with the police by contacting their lawyers in advance and giving them their medical records. They thus reduced their personal fears which would otherwise make the action unacceptable. Activists also divided into groups and visited poor neighbourhoods to motivate them to join the protests (Ozgul, 2019). In line with Frijda (2004) and Bandura's (1977, p. 193) theories, their past actions motivated them to think that protesting was acceptable and available, and that the potential outcome was worth the risks.

Frijda's third motivation is the perceived urgency and importance of the emotions experienced witnessing the event that drives protest action. The more intense the emotion, coupled with recognition that the event has personal implications, the greater the perceived urgency and importance of acting. In the video that triggered the BLM protests, the public saw an unarmed black man, George Floyd, pleading helplessly for his life until he died due to the pressure applied by the police on his neck. Witnessing someone die in such a brutal and unjust way will likely stimulate strong emotional responses, particularly anger and sadness, but these do not directly lead to action (Jasper, 1998, p. 399). Disgust, as well as fear among those from black communities who have experienced racism and felt they could be George Floyd, intensified their urgency to take to the streets (Le Poidevin, 2020). For example, Omer Reshid, a high school student, expressed that

> ever since the video [of George Floyd's killing], a lot of us, especially African Americans, have been feeling very angry and frustrated, but also scared. I know, for me, as a Black man, it is only a matter of time until I face racial discrimination that is going to lead me to put myself in a situation that has my life on the line and that is really scary to me.
>
> (Bryant, 2020)

Black citizens felt a strong association with the treatment meted out to Floyd and felt the necessity to take action. That Floyd had also recently lost his job due to the Covid-19 stay at home order, a situation in which denial of a packet of cigarettes due to the suspicion that is $20 dollar bill was a forgery, was something with which many Americans could sympathise. According to a Pew Research Centre survey (2020), the majority of white Americans (60%) expressed some support for the BLM movement. All these factors made many feel it was urgent and important to make their voices heard before what happened to Floyd happened to them.

The final condition relates to social norms, beliefs, and values, which Frijda defined as the social eye. Protest is a public action; citizens are likely to consider whether participation conforms to the social values and norms of the society in which they live. Those first engaging in a protest movement may use their immediate community as a reference point. However, as a protest movement grows, as in the case of BLM, seeing other citizens participating can act as a motivational force: to protest becomes the norm. Social media provides important spaces for social norms to be defined. On Instagram, millions posted a black square tagged with #Blackouttuesday to show their support for BLM. TV channels and radio programs changed their programs to mark #blackouttuesday (Bakare & Davies, 2020). Societal support for the protests put pressure on those who supported the aims of the protest but had hitherto stayed silent and led the participants in the protest to expand. Hence, footage of the protests offered vicarious experiences which increased the self-efficacy of would-be participants (Bandura, 1977). US citizens are also familiar with protests, they are acceptable, available and the frequent response to injustices which are seen as important and to which a response is urgently necessary. BLM protesters will have witnessed the #MeToo protests which emerged in the US in 2006, when the phrase was coined by founder Tarana Burke, which highlight instances of sexual harassment and abuse and ultimately campaigned for ending the misuse of power and privilege. Given the similarity between the Me Too and BLM objectives (Gill & Rahman-Jones, 2020), and the prominence and success of Me Too, the barriers to participating in BLM protests became minimal and, like Me Too, BLM became a global phenomenon during May 2020.

There are specific circumstances around the pandemic that may also have led to greater numbers of participants. Some may have sought an excuse to leave their homes, congregate with others and viewed this as a virtuous way to use up free time. Others may have wished to vent anger and frustration at their situation due to restrictions on economic and social life. However, choosing this protest, wishing to be part of a movement making a statement about Floyd's death, also has an emotion dimension that relates directly to that event. Floyd's death provided the urgency and importance. But the event also made congregating acceptable and rather than the 'social eye' opposing mass gatherings, they were made more acceptable due to the importance and emotional resonance of the event. Protest is perhaps the most dramatic form of political participation, and therefore requires a greater motivational push, however we argue that all forms of political participation are considered to some extent and we move to the alternative end of the spectrum to discuss online activism.

## THE SLACKTIVISM DEBATE

Notwithstanding the prominence of protests such as MeToo and BLM in recent years we have seen a steady decline in the number of people active in various forms of political participation, particularly voting, to which we devote attention later in the chapter. In particular, many young people pursue value-driven issues through non-parliamentary means. They are at the forefront of the Occupy Movement, US tighter gun control campaigns, environmental protection, women's rights, LGBTQ rights, anti-war movements etc. They do not see these values represented by mainstream parties and so young people are less likely to vote than older people (Sloam & Henn, 2019, p. 119). For example, in the last 2019 UK elections, 74% of those aged 65+ voted in the 2019 UK election, but only 47% of 18 to 24-year-olds voted (The House of Commons Library, 2019).

What is happening is not a decline in political engagement, defined as having interest in issues which are political. Citizens, particularly 18 to 24-year-olds, prefer to engage in what are considered non-traditional forms of political participation such as engaging with information on websites, weblogs or social media platforms (Koc Michalska et al., 2013; Lilleker, 2014, p. 152). Such actions are often considered to be low effort, as they involve activities such as liking and sharing content. Technological determinists call these forms of online participation 'slacktivism': feel good online activism with zero political or social impact (Morozov, 2012). These online participation methods are often deemed to involve minimal financial or emotional risks and, critics argue, to convert slacktivists into activists willing to take high-risk action, such as the Movement for Black Lives, is challenging and requires strategy (Gladwell, 2010). For instance, the 2011 Syrian peaceful protests showed that, even though the protesters brought together an army of supporters on the 'Syrian Revolution 2011' Facebook page, when the admins called for participation in a protest, only experienced activists joined them in the offline sphere. The motivational dimensions cited by Frijda such as availability (i.e. past protest experiences and tactics) can only be acquired at sites of protest. Due to the fact that the Facebook users did not know what to expect in a protest, they did not join the protests (Ozgul, 2019).

However, what the technological determinists often neglect is the dialectical relationship between online and offline political engagement. Unlike the first attempt to organise a protest by the Syrian Revolution Facebook page admins, the protest organisers often switch between the digital and non-digital communication tools while organising an action (Theocharis, 2015). They use both digital media and conventional communication methods such as interpersonal communication. They also distribute brochures and statements about the protests and give interviews to the traditional media channels (Aouragh & Alexander, 2011; Ozgul, 2019).

The communication strategies of campaign organisations are seen as of significant importance for drawing people closer to the organisation and making them more prepared to engage in activism. In adapting the consumer loyalty ladder, Lilleker and Jackson (2014) suggested communication should resonate with those who might engage and provide ways they can discover further information which should be designed to draw those who find the issue salient closer to the campaign. To accomplish this, the organisers should know their target audience well and adopt their language and forms of expression. For instance, when the 'Syrian Revolution 2011' Facebook page administrators used religious expressions and illustrations in their posts, these created reservations in the minds of some Syrians (Ozgul, 2019, p. 139). While joining online discussion or supportive groups are expressions of interest and passive support, engaging in supportive activities online indicates a stronger commitment. Campaigns must increase the salience of the issue and the urgency of action to encourage those within a supportive community to be more active and become evangelists, promoting the campaign online and offline and becoming activists.

Hence, to make social media users overcome their fears and be more likely to follow a repertoire of activism, protest organisers often initially invite supporters to take part in low effort, less risky actions, those often dismissed as clicktivism. Prior to the 2011 protests in Egypt, the 'Kullena Khaled Said' Facebook page was launched to raise awareness of police repression. The page particularly aimed to engage the reluctant middle-class. By publicising the page, creating content relevant and salient for a middle-class audience and encouraging liking and sharing of content, the page moved to organise silent stands. Participants were asked to wear black and stand in the streets to show their opposition to the state. This low effort, low risk action built a stronger sense of unity and community as well as a sense of self-efficacy among participants that they could bring about change through political activism. The protesters hence acquired the second motivational determinant in the Frijda's list: availability of a repertoire (Ozgul, 2019, p. 83).

Unity and community were also not built overnight in the movement behind BLM. Even before its emergence, police brutality and racism were hot topics in the US public sphere, creating a network of activists and the emergence of spontaneous protests (Jackson et al., 2020). In 2012, when Trayvon Martin was killed by police officer George Zimmerman, an online petition was launched demanding Zimmerman's indictment. This gathered 10,000 signatures in just a few days, including high profile celebrities (Jackson et al., 2020). In the wake of the petition, protesters filled the streets across the US chanting "we are all Trayvon Martin". As a sign of solidarity, many celebrities and athletes posed in hooded sweatshirts to protest the killing of Martin, who also wore a hoodie on the day of his death. All these previous, often low effort, forms of online and offline political engagements have built unity and community and developed the repertoire of the BLM movement.

## THE AFFECTIVE VALUE OF CLICKS, LIKES AND SHARES

The actions Morozov dismisses as clicktivism, however, are not purely gateway actions to a wider activist repertoire. Papacharissi (2016) argues that sharing online hashtags such as #Blacklivesmatter or #Handsupdontshoot are both a form of affective expression as well a form of connective action (Bennett & Segerberg, 2013); they are an expression of emotional support and a way of communities expressing solidarity with one another. An affect is the "pre-emotive intensity people experience prior to cognitively ascribing an emotional label to a sentiment" (Papacharissi, 2016). It is the intensity felt just as when we hear a song we like, environmental stimuli which produce affects cause a measurable change in our bodies: a quickened heart rate, higher brain wave activity, hormone release etc. An affect is felt as pain, joy and love, powerful emotions which one might need to act upon (Papacharissi, 2015).

As the photos of both protesters and repressive police action spread online, conversations across social media channels connected by hashtags such as #BlackLivesMatter invite affective engagement

(Papacharissi, 2016). Social media channels such as Twitter permit users to share their personal points of view and collate their personal perspectives into connective narratives. The BLM movement supporters, for instance, raised awareness of police repression and racial discrimination by expressing their negative perceptions, reactions and feelings about racial violence. These activities amplify marginalised voices, spread them virally through public networks and intensify public debate (Shirky, 2010; Dennis, 2019, p. 51). Twitter users also communicate with others to seek and provide psychosocial support around issues of racial inequality (De Choudry et al., 2017). While synchronising their thoughts, they also "reciprocally stimulate their emotions, thus engendering a collective effervescence" (Garcia & Rime, 2019). Affective engagement with online content thus intensifies participants' sense of social identity and belonging within a community of like-minded others. Social media pages act as channels of contestation and solidarity around which communities form. Channels of contestation appear when social media users challenge hegemonic ideas. The feelings of solidarity emerge as users join around a hashtag such as #MeToo or #BlackLivesMatter (Shirky, 2010; Dennis, 2019, p. 51). As the social media users come together, they form bonds of sentiments, their feelings towards the issue become more intense and they perceive the protests as more important. As use of hashtags increases within a society, they are further motivated to protest and their hopes for achieving their objectives increase. Social media users can thus acquire at least three out of the four motivational dimensions necessary for action on social media: acceptability, urgency and the social eye.

Overall, the four motivational factors cited previously may induce people to change their attitudes and intentions. The intentions are important as people act in accordance with them. Behavioural psychologist Ajzen (1991) explains their importance by arguing that to perform any one form of action, one must first have positive attitudes towards the specific behaviour and the efficacy of that behaviour to have a high propensity to perform that action. The availability of the four motivational factors cited by Frijda induce an individual to positively evaluate a behaviour. For instance, if would-be protesters believe the outcome of an action is an acceptable risk to them, there will be higher likelihood of action. Not only the acceptability of that action but Ajzen's theory of planned behaviour (1991) claims the perceived efficacy of behaviour is also important. As mentioned previously, protesters' familiarity with an action increases their self-efficacy. Protesters feel more capable to perform a protest if they have past protest experiences and networks. What protesters learn from their past actions also makes them feel more capable to handle future obstacles. Furthermore, Ajzen (1991) also argues that one may seek validation from others, close peers or those whose opinion is respected to calculate whether performing the action may incur rewards or punishments. This motivational determinant is also emphasised by Frijda's social eye dimension. For instance, as their close peers on social media reward their pictures or posts with likes or other emojis, the protesters may feel more motivated to read and share political content. The size of a user's network can also be perceived as a reward and so encourage forms of behaviours. The rewards of peers, the social eye, thus shapes intentions to perform actions. Finally, Ajzen (1991) highlights a final motivational determinant that develops Frijda's theory (2004), the control beliefs. In his theory of planned behaviour, drawn from health campaign research, control focused on the ability to perform a behaviour. For example, an individual can accept that smoking is bad for their health and that those they care about think they should stop smoking; however, the power of the addiction may override these considerations. There may be practical barriers to attending protests or other forms of political participation, however a more serious barrier is not solely about performing an action but the extent to which the action is likely to have a positive outcome (Lilleker, 2014). A person may feel that protesting is an important part of democratic life and know their close peers are also going, however they may feel the effort of attending is not worth it as the target of the protest, usually the government, will not listen. Alternatively, a person can feel a duty to vote and be from a family who habitually votes, but see none of the viable candidates as sharing their values or a political vision they wish to see implemented. Hence, a lack of control over an outcome can lead to apathy and reduce the propensity to participate.

## VOTING

Voting is perhaps both the most studied but also most opaque form of political participation. Any individual vote is unlikely to have any impact on the outcome, hence logically, voting is perhaps the least efficacious form of political participation. Yet, if sufficient people turn out and vote the same way, they will determine who will govern their nation, so voting has significant power. But in every democracy the political system is fraught with problems that can depress voter turnout. Therefore, we consider why is it people vote and how they make their decisions.

Lilleker (2014) argues that four factors may determine the likelihood that an individual will vote or not. Firstly, whether they view voting as their duty as a democratic citizen, a factor that often seems to be stronger in women than men. Secondly, there is the question of whether voting is viewed as empowering, or put another way, whether the person's vote is likely to have any tangible or symbolic impact. Tangible effects relate to impacts on the outcome of the contest, while symbolic effects denote the act of voting for a party that is unlikely to win but regardless, there is a desire to register support. Thirdly, the voting processes must be perceived to be fair; if not, then many may view their vote as a waste and voting to be a waste of time. Finally, is the election contest inspirational and does one candidate or party inspire an individual to at minimum make the effort to cast their vote?

The latter factor, which determines the choice of whether to vote, in turn will govern the extent that one engages with the contest and segues neatly into a discussion of voter choices. Even the most dutiful voter may struggle to decide how to cast their vote; some will resort to habit or may simply decide which is the least bad option. Others may spoil their ballot papers to show their protest against the lack of real choice. However, in mapping voter decision making to Ajzen's theory of planned behaviour, Lilleker proposes that first a voter must develop some interest in one or more of the campaigns of parties or candidates and secondly, as a result, must develop a desire for one party's programme to be implemented. These, along with the factors previously described, shape the attitudes towards voting. Thirdly and fourthly, voters may seek to ascertain whether their choice is reinforced by their peers, perhaps through face-to-face conversations or monitoring their friends' political chats on social networks. Voters may also explore if there are independent endorsements of their choice, perhaps from trusted media, celebrities or experts. These factors form referent beliefs that affirm an individual's choice. Finally, there are two factors which might determine whether the voters feel they can achieve their objectives. If we assume that no citizen is excluded from voting, a factor true for every well-functioning democracy which excludes citizens from voting along limited and clearly defined parameters, then voters may calculate what likelihood there is of their chosen party or candidate being elected. If the answer is that the favourite party is unlikely to win, and if a symbolic vote is seen as pointless, this can lead to a depression of the vote or them to employ tactical voting to attempt to prevent one party from winning. Trust, however, is also a factor. One might find the policies of one party or candidate very appealing, however, can they or the system ensure these policies are implemented? Hence, the likelihood of a party implementing its programme may be a calculation that determines voting. This discussion suggests that voters monitor the landscape of an election, perhaps adopting a degree of passivity towards the contest. Amnå and Ekman (2014) suggest that the four faces of political passivity are active (6%), standby (45%), unengaged (27%) and disillusioned (22%). The number of active citizens may be low, as Amnå and Ekman estimate them to represent about 6%. Standby citizens stay alert, keep informed and will participate when it is deemed important for them. The unengaged may be those who have previously been inspired but let down, or who feel completely unrepresented by any of the parties or candidates standing. The disillusioned may vary depending on the extent that they find the contest inspiring, like the programme of one or more of the competitors and feel that the programme is likely to be implemented. Largely, all but the active are on standby, awaiting to feel some degree of arousal as a result of their exposure to the contest.

## ISSUE VOTING

Issues are a key source of arousal, as often people care more about a small number of policy areas than an entire programme. Voters in the first round of the 2017 French presidential elections found that the traditional system of left and right blocs had weakened, hence they were driven to vote along issue lines and be guided by the salience and resonance of campaign messaging. Research shows that voters of the far-right Front Nationale were likely to be blue-collar workers, have lower job stability, lack higher educational achievement and hold higher levels of anti-establishment, anti-EU and anti-immigration positions. The salience and resonance of the promises to protect unskilled jobs by Marine Le Pen's Front Nationale eroded support from the far-left grouping led by Jean-Luc Mélenchon. The more centre-right grouping of François Fillon and the socialist party of Benoît Hamon, both ridden by division and plagued by scandal, were in turn undermined by the candidature of Emmanuel Macron and his centrist En Marche! His value positions were the polar opposite of those of Le Pen. The second round thus saw Le Pen and Macron offer very clear choices to the French voters, Macron won due to there being a greater support for a more inclusivist, globalist and pro-European programme. He also benefitted from the *cordon sanitaire* which has traditionally meant voters will look to whoever is opposing Front Nationale to exclude that party from the presidency or dominance in parliament. However, the first round also demonstrates that those within society who experience a more precarious existence, with low job security and fewer opportunities for economic or social mobility, are turning to more populist, extremist and authoritarian candidates or programmes (Evans & Ivaldi, 2017). These trends resonate with the findings of research into which UK voters were most likely to vote for Brexit and which US voters were most likely to endorse Trump.

Sloam and Henn (2019) suggest an interesting schism which links well to the work of Inglehart and others discussed in Chapter 1. Researching voting intentions in the UK, they argue that voters can be separated into two groups: materialists and post-materialists. The former tends to be similar to the voters we describe previously who voted for Brexit in the UK in 2016, Trump in the US the same year and Le Pen to be French president in 2017. Post-materialists however are a more complex group. In particular, young post-materialists tend to be more disillusioned with the remoteness of democratic institutions and will act as stand-by citizens when considering participation in elections. These voters may turn out to block the advance of the far right, particularly if they support the programme of the alternative, but largely tend to pursue extra-parliamentary forms of action (Sloam & Henn, 2019, p. 30).

Young post-materialists are at the forefront of social movements that promote greater equality and environmental protection, suggesting they possess fairly strong values which they find are not represented by mainstream parties (Sloam & Henn, 2019, p. 119). Sloam and Henn found that post-materialist values were a strong predictor for voting to remain in the EU in the UK in 2016, mirroring the policy positions that led a similar group to support Macron in France in 2017. In the US in 2016 and 2020 younger voters may have been pivotal. Young voters felt Hillary Clinton lacked the strength of character or empathy to be a leader and believed her to be dishonest; they thus mostly made their judgement based on the image and characteristics of Clinton rather than her issue position. Young voters did not have similar negative views towards Donald Trump and were not wholly turned off by his more extreme policies. It is likely however that their dislike for Clinton, and unless they were particularly engaged by Trump's messaging, caused a greater propensity to not vote, contributing to the continued decline of the youth vote in the US.

The US 2020 election coincided with the global crisis that was the Covid-19 pandemic. Some nations have witnessed a longer and deeper crisis than others and the US is one. The pandemic exposed weaknesses in fragile or failing democracies (Lilleker et al., 2021) but also in some advanced democracies. The 2020 US presidential election saw two contrasting campaigns and candidates vying for office, with Democrat Joe Biden emerging as the winner, consigning Republican Donald Trump to joining the short list of one term presidents. Biden amassed a broad coalition of voters. He could not win a majority among white men or women, but overwhelmingly won the support of the Black and Latino communities. He also won a majority among voters whose households earned less than $100,000 per annum. Given the 7 million vote margin between Biden and Trump, two things were pivotal. Firstly, and based on the mathematics, Biden managed to convert some 5 million voters who voted for Trump in 2016. Secondly, Biden gained around 2 million extra votes from the increase in average turnout of 6.7%, around 2 million voters. In particular, in states Biden flipped, the increase in turnout in Michigan was 64.69% in 2016 but 73.9% in 2020; in Wisconsin turnout was 68.33% in 2016 but 75.8% in 2020. Biden won more votes than any previous candidate for the presidency, 12 million more than Clinton in 2016 and 9 million more than Obama in 2008. Trump, however, also increased his vote share by 10 million from 2016. Hence, there was definitely an increase in turnout, and in particular, from certain communities most likely to vote Democrat. These were motivated by the opportunity to reject Trump's values and policy stance and by the belief their vote would make a difference. The latter can be explained by the significant increases in turnout in states where historically, there are small margins between Republicans and Democrats. The former is explained by focusing on the reasons given in the exit polls for voting decisions which elide well with post-materialist values.

Biden voters overwhelmingly supported dealing with the pandemic over protecting the economy. They were also in favour of ending racial inequities. The binary choice seems simple: if you cared about dealing with the pandemic, health care policy generally and racial inequality, you voted for Biden; if your concerns were the economy and crime you voted for Trump. Given that BLM protests were framed as a criminal activity by Trump, the big differences between the 78% concerned about crime who voted Trump and the 91% who cared about racial inequality who voted for Biden were clear on this issue alone. The issues that Sloam and Henn found to be important among post-materialist voters are health care, economy, housing, education, Europe, environment, immigration and asylum. While not all of these map onto the most important issues among voters in the US in 2020, in the context of a pandemic, the fit is remarkable. What divides materialists from post-materialists is perspective. Post-materialists approach these issues from a more inclusive and communitarian perspective, welcoming immigrants and wishing to share current benefits enjoyed in Western societies with the broader global community while focusing on protecting the world for future generations. In contrast, materialists approach politics from a more personalised perspective. They view the world in a more zero-sum way and any sharing of the benefits within a society is seen as a risk to their access to those benefits, hence immigrants are viewed as competitors from outside as opposed to being equal members of a community. Hence, the motivations for voting differ markedly between these two groups and when the vote matters, and can make a difference, post-materialists can be drawn to the ballot box.

Democracies require citizens to be active and participatory. However, citizens require the motivations to engage with democratic processes. They must feel that the form of participation is available, acceptable, is important and that the social eye is supportive of the action. Thus, political campaigns must provide the stimuli that engages citizens, if not, they will remain on standby and largely disinterested. Protesting and voting are complex activities, both of crucial importance. Protests bring awareness of injustices and inequities to a wider audience. Voting determines who makes the decisions which shape the future of a country. But to take part in either, citizens must feel that they have the potential not only to be heard but to be listened to and so to be influential. Social media offers a gateway into activism, but also a means for activists to mobilise others. It is a space that can allow citizens with strong feelings on issues, some which may not be effectively represented in national parliaments, to find their communities and develop repertoires of activism. These all provide the bases from which political participation can flourish. However, perceptions of the state of democracy, and the tone set by national leaders, matter enormously. Leaders can mobilise voters, create the conditions for protest and for revolution and can inspire or suppress engagement. 2020 has been a year of sharp contrasts in the way that citizens feel about their nations, their democracies and their leaders and as a post-script to this discussion, we consider the contrasting outcomes not for the pandemic or for people—they are important stories to be told elsewhere. In the concluding chapter, we sketch out how voters think about democracies while also considering how the pandemic has impacted on democracies and exposed their weaknesses.

## REFERENCES

Ajzen, I. (1991). The theory of planned behavior. *Organizational Behavior and Human Decision Processes*, 50(2), 179–211. https://doi.org/10.1016/0749-5978(91)90020-T

Amnå, E., & Ekman, J. (2014). Standby citizens: Diverse faces of political passivity. *European Political Science Review*, 6(2), 261–281. https://doi.org/10.1017/S175577391300009X

Aouragh, M., & Alexander, A. (2011). The Arab Spring: The Egyptian experience: Sense and nonsense of the Internet revolution. *International Journal of Communication*, 5, 1344–1358.

Bakare, L., & Davies, C. (2020, June 2). Blackout Tuesday: Black squares dominate social media and spark debate. *The Guardian*. https://bit.ly/3472OCm

Bandura, A. (1977). Self-efficacy: Toward a unifying theory of behavioral change. *Psychological Review*, 84(2), 191–215. https://doi.org/10.1016/0146-6402(78)90002-4

Bryant, M. (2020, June 15). "It was time to take charge": The Black youth leading the George Floyd protests. *The Guardian*. www.theguardian.com/world/2020/jun/15/black-youth-activism-george-floyd-protests

Davou, B., & Demertzis, N. (2013). Feeling the Greek financial crisis. In N. Demertzis (Ed.), *Emotions in politics* (pp. 93–123). Palgrave Macmillan. https://doi.org/10.1057/9781137025661_6

De Choudry, M., Shagun, J., Benjamin, S., & Ingmar, W. (2017). Social media participation in an activist movement for racial equality. *Proceedings of the International AAAI Conference on Weblogs and Social Media*, 92–101. www.ncbi.nlm. nih.gov/pmc/articles/PMC5565729/

Dennis, J. (2019). *Beyond slacktivism: Political participation on social media*. Palgrave Macmillan. https://doi.org/10.1007/978-3-030-00844-4

Evans, J., & Ivaldi, G. (2017). *The 2017 French presidential elections: A political reformation?* Palgrave Macmillan. https://doi.org/10.1007/978-3-319-68327-0

Frijda, N. (2004). Emotions and action. In A. Manstead, N. Frijda, & A. Fischer (Eds.), *Studies in emotion and social interaction. Feelings and emotions: The Amsterdam symposium* (pp. 158–173). Cambridge University Press. https://doi. org/10.1017/CBO9780511806582.010

Garcia, D., & Rime, B. (2019). Collective emotions and social resilience in the digital traces after a terrorist attack. *Psychological Science*, 30(4), 617–628. https://doi.org/10.1177/0956797619831964

Ghonim, W. (2012). *Revolution 2.0*. Fourth Estate.

Gill G., & Rahman-Jones, I. (2020, July 9). Me too founder Tarana Burke: Movement is not over. *BBC*. www.bbc.co.uk/news/newsbeat-53269751

Gladwell, M. (2010, October 4). Small change: Why the revolution will not be tweeted. *The New Yorker*. www.newyorker.com/magazine/2010/10/04/ small-change-malcolm-gladwell

The House of Commons Library (2019). *General election 2019: Turnout*. https://commonslibrary.parliament.uk/general-election-2019-turnout/

Jackson, S. J., Bailey, M., & Brooke, F. W. (2020). *#Hashtag activism: Networks of race and gender justice*. The MIT Press.

Jasper, J. M. (1998). Social movements. *Sociological Forum*, 13(3), 397–424.

Koc Michalska, K., Lilleker, D. G., & Suroweic, P. (2013). The use of the web for political participation. In A. Charles (Ed.), *Media/democracy: A comparative study* (pp. 81–102). Cambridge Scholarly Publishing.

Leach W. C., & Allen M. A. (2017). The social psychology of the Black lives matter meme and movement. *Current Directions in Psychological Science*, 26(6), 543–547. https://doi.org/10.1177/0963721417719319

Le Poidevin, O. (2020, June 8). George Floyd: Black lives matter protests go global. *BBC*. www.bbc.co.uk/news/av/world-52967551

Lilleker, D. G. (2014). *Political communication and cognition*. Palgrave Macmillan. https://doi.org/10.1057/9781137313430

Lilleker, D. G., & Jackson, N. (2014). Brand management and relationship marketing in online environments. In J. Lees-Marshment, B. Conley, & K. Cosgrove (Eds.), *Political marketing in the United States* (pp. 165–184). Routledge.

Lilleker, D., Coman, I. A., Gregor, M., & Novelli, E. (Eds.). (2021). Political Communication and COVID-19: Governance and Rhetoric in Times of Crisis. Routledge.

Morozov, E. (2012). *The net delusion: How not to liberate the world.* Penguin.

Papacharissi, Z. (2015). *Affective publics: Sentiment, technology, and politics.* Oxford University Press. https://doi.org/10.1093/acprof:oso/9780199999736.001.0001

Papacharissi, Z. (2016). Trump and publics of affect. *Medium.* https://medium.com/@zizip/trump-and-publics-of-affect-514716c4a79f

Pew Research Center (2020). *Amid protests, majorities across racial and ethnic groups express support for the Black lives matter movement.* www.pewsocialtrends.org/2020/06/12/amid-protests-majorities-across-racial-and-ethnic-groups-express-support-for-the-black-lives-matter-movement/

Shirky, C. (2010). *Here comes everybody.* Penguin.

Theocharis, Y. (2015). The conceptualization of digitally networked participation. *Social Media + Society, 1*(2). https://doi.org/10.1177/2056305115610140

## FURTHER READING

Bennett, W. L., & Segerberg, A. (2013). *The logic of connective action: Digital media and the personalization of contentious politics.* Cambridge University Press. https://doi.org/10.1080/1369118X.2012.670661

Frijda, N. H. (1986). *The emotions.* Cambridge University Press.

Ozgul, A. B. (2019). *Leading protests in the digital age: Youth activism in Egypt and Syria.* Palgrave Macmillan. https://doi.org/10.1007/978-3-030-25450-6

Sloam, J., & Henn, M. (2019). *Youthquake 2017.* Palgrave Macmillan. https://doi.org/10.1007/978-3-319-97469-9

# 5

## UNDERSTANDING THE PSYCHOLOGY OF CONTEMPORARY DEMOCRACIES

A strong and healthy democracy does not only depend on the electoral process or the functioning of government, but also the confidence of citizens in democratic institutions. Citizens need to trust in the institutions of democracy and feel they have some degree of power and influence over them. What political scientists often neglect to ask is, what determines the extent that citizens trust democratic institutions? Why do some citizens feel more trusting of democratic institutions than others? This book explores these issues and argues that the way that citizens understand and engage with their political systems is, first of all, contingent on their identities and values. The experiences of citizens with their caregivers, their significant others, their education as well as their ethnic, religious and social background all shape their identities and values. The first chapter also explains that the communication and actions of political organisations, citizens' experiences of interactions with political outputs and the mediation of politics also interact with their identities and values. In other words, citizens assess the extent that how the system operates, and the outputs from the system, conform to their hopes and expectations. Meeting hopes and expectations results in trust and satisfaction and, while we cannot expect 100% trust and satisfaction, we should not find 100% mistrust and dissatisfaction in a functioning

DOI: 10.4324/9781003021292-5

democracy. In reality, citizens perhaps sit somewhere on a scale on both dimensions, trusting but sceptical and partially satisfied. Where they sit on these scales will determine their cognitive processes and will shape the general emotional state within a nation.

Our discussion of cognitive processes in Chapter 2 has emphasised the different ways in which lived experiences such as the economic crisis can shape identities and values and cognitive interactions with political institutions. In highlighting how some can feel marginalised, despite living in a society where principles of equality can be enshrined in legislation, we show how some citizens can come to believe that the democratic processes do not work for them and so lack legitimacy. This is important as it suggests some sections of society are far closer to having almost no trust or satisfaction in the political system.

Significant challenges are posed to democracies by the emergence of highly polarised positions which can become reinforced in citizens through a desire for their biases and prejudices to be confirmed. Drawing on contemporary examples, in Chapter 2 we illustrate how citizens often prefer to believe they have sufficient knowledge and that their beliefs are innately correct and make generalisations while engaging with or selecting new information. The retreat into echo chambers can lead to the development of even more extreme beliefs and the adoption of a position that is anti-democratic. The widespread usage of digital media and communication from parties and campaigns can exacerbate these issues, as well as encourage citizens to engage superficially. Extreme beliefs reinforce negative perspectives of 'the system' and towards those with alternative perspectives and undermine the pluralist principles on which democracies operate. While personal and group identities are becoming blurred, group members become reluctant to question the dominant group narrative. When this narrative does not conform with the dominant narrative in the country, the decline in trust in democratic institutions become inevitable.

We discuss another significant challenge to democracies posed by the use of digital media in Chapter 3: the flow of simplistic messages.

Simplistic messages are important, as instead of carefully and critically evaluating a message, individuals often form their judgements based on these simplistic cues. The flow of simplistic messages may lead to the formation of strong attitudes, but these attitudes may not be well informed. Our discussion exposes a tension at the heart of democracy relating to political communication. Politicians seek to appear close and relevant to their citizens, but in order to ensure citizens understand and recall their messages, they must keep the message simple. Hence, citizens are more likely to be ill-informed, driven more by beliefs than well-informed attitudes and to have gut reactions based on lived experiences interacting with exposure to simple image-based arguments. This situation is incompatible with the core principles of democracy.

Political participation can be seen therefore as the result of gut reactions. The increase in protests all around the world reflects a declining trust towards politicians. As the simplistic messages of politicians fail to address the economic and social problems of their countries and the lived experiences of citizens, mass protests have been witnessed around the world since 2009, as the impact of the economic crash was felt. In Chapter 4, we show that joining a protest is not simply based on an emotional reaction to external stimulus. In order for citizens to engage in collective action, the action needs to be familiar to them, involve acceptable levels of personal risk, be perceived as urgent and important and conform to their social values and norms. Through the analysis of recent protests such as those under the BLM banner, we show how these motivational factors were available for protesters in different countries. We also discuss the value of social media in terms of raising awareness, stimulating emotions and generating collective effervescence. Today, many citizens may participate in actions that they believe are available, accessible and acceptable and that may have some positive impact for their lives. However, many also remain disengaged. It is becoming more important than ever to understand why there is a decline in the number of people who participate in traditional forms of political action such as voting. In Chapter 4, we discuss the four motivational factors affecting an individual's likelihood to vote and argue that in order to vote, a citizen must first view voting as a democratic duty and believe he/she will have a tangible impact on the outcome. The voting process must also be perceived to be fair and the citizens must feel inspired by one candidate or party. Drawing on the presidential elections in France and the US, we demonstrate how voters were driven by the issue position and/or images of political candidates. Non-participants, on the other hand, believe voting offers little benefit to them.

The inequities in engagement and in trust and the inconsistencies between the principles of democracy and the practices of political communication have never been exposed in the same way as they have in 2020 as a result of the Covid-19 pandemic. Drawing on theories discussed in the previous chapters, this concluding chapter examines the human impulses and drivers that have shaped nation-specific attitudes towards democracy during the pandemic and offers solutions to tackle the challenges that democratic institutions currently face.

## DEMOCRACY IN LOCKDOWN

2020 was a year of contradictions. It was a year when many citizens of democracies rallied around the flag in a national effort to beat the Covid-19 virus and awarded greater support to their leaders. Despite lockdowns, some citizens took to the streets in support of Black Lives Matter. Other citizens went out to protest the restrictions brought in to reduce the spread of the virus. The unprecedented restriction of freedom and mobility impacted the psychology of many societies and accentuated the problems at the heart of democratic systems. In April 2020, statistica.com estimated that one third of the 8 billion population of the planet were under lockdown conditions and by summer 2020 the estimate rose to a quarter. In February 2021, every single nation remained affected and enduring severe restrictions. The measures to control movement ranged from being heavily policed, not only in authoritarian regimes such as China, but also in France and Italy. Elsewhere, compliance with restrictions was brought in as strong government or state advisory policies with lighter touch policing, in particular the UK and USA. Some democratically elected leaders dismissed the threat of the Covid-19 virus; Brazilian president Jair Bolsonaro described it as 'a little flu' and the response of other nations and the World Health Organisation as 'hysterical'. The response of US president Trump foreshadowed his rejection by voters concerned about the spread and impact of Covid-19. He at different points called it a 'hoax', labelled it the Chinese virus, made wearing face masks a partisan issue, and while later acknowledging the threat, prioritised the economy when calling for state governors to relax restrictions. The differing responses are symptomatic to a degree of the style of leaders, the extent they prioritise human life over national economic interests as well as their preparedness for coping with a pandemic of this magnitude.

The public responses to the measures are further indicative of differing national attitudes towards the democracy and the legitimacy of their governments (Lilleker et al., 2021). In this book, we show that trust in institutions might increase or decrease based on emotional factors such as feelings of belonging, empowerment and of representation. Hence, the measures taken by governments during the pandemic required citizens to view the restrictions as appropriate, necessary and legitimate requests. New Zealand is hailed as the nation which restricted the spread of the virus and deaths most successfully (Boland, 2020). With only 102 confirmed cases on March 23 2020, the Health Minister announced the country would be at Alert Level 3, implementing social distancing and restricting movement. With cases doubling to 205 by March 25, lockdown was implemented and all but essential businesses were forced to close. Previously, Prime Minister Jacinda Ardern managed to bring solidarity and social cohesion when New Zealand faced a white supremacist attack on its Muslim community. Ardern successfully unified her citizens against the attack while showing solidarity with the Muslim community. During the pandemic, while there was some disquiet among business owners regarding the definition of essential business, a combination of daily briefings from Ardern and fulsome support from the media again ensured social cohesion, widescale compliance and no serious challenges.

Contrasting styles, and the perceptions they offer, perhaps explain different public responses. While UK Prime Minister Boris Johnson pre-recorded his March 24 2020 lockdown announcement and did not provide the media opportunities to ask questions, Ardern gave extensive time for media questions during her lockdown announcement, demonstrating a dedication to transparency and desire to allay concerns (Wilson, 2020). Prior to the lockdown on 21–22 March 2020, Utting Research found that 62% of New Zealanders were satisfied with the government response, this increased to 84% in a small poll conducted by Colmar Brunton on 3–5 April, and 87% in a poll conducted by the same company on 20–21 April 2020. New Zealand instituted a phased return to normalcy on 27 April 2020, with the country having only 1,479 confirmed cases and 19 deaths. Like many other democracies, in September 2020, data showed the GDP of New Zealand had fallen by 12.2%. However, despite economic recession, citizens continued to have trust in their leader (Graham-McLay, 2020). Symbolic acts of proximity played a role. Ardern and other ministers took a 20% pay cut to show their solidarity with those hit by the pandemic. They thus displayed understanding of the challenges citizens faced and signalled their solidarity with them. Ardern has consistently polled well for personal popularity during her leadership of the minority coalition, overcoming the challenges of partnering in government with the nationalist and populist New Zealand First and managing the supply and demand supportive relationship with the Greens. Ardern's inclusive approach allowed her to bridge divisions in politics and the country. Thus, her standing and reputation meant she was trusted handling the crisis. Her reputation was enhanced as she won plaudits from the global media for managing the Covid-19 crisis. The result has been that Ardern won a majority in parliament for her Labour Party in the October 2020 election.

Contrasting this with the US, a federal system where the president may set the general tone and speaks to and for the whole nation, but state governors are the arbiters of more local measures.

Trump's message has oscillated between dismissal and acceptance of the severity of the Covid-19 threat, at points contradicting the advice of health experts and publicly opposing instituting the state of emergency on March 13 2020. Measures taken across states differed markedly. New York, the state with most cases, California where the first death occurred and Illinois issued stay at home orders on 15–21 March 2020 and a raft of other states followed over the next four-weeks, although a small number of states including North and South Dakota, Iowa, Nebraska and Utah instituted no restrictions whatso-ever. The contrasting messages at the national and state levels, and inconsistencies have led to high levels of public uncertainty and pro-tests in many states. The inconsistencies are evident. Wyoming, with 559 cases and seven deaths, closed bars, clubs and theatres, restricted gatherings to nine or less people and advised only essential move-ment. In contrast, Iowa had 7,000 confirmed cases and 162 deaths and only restricted public gatherings, issuing no stay-at-home orders. Protests have been witnessed across a range of states, challenging the measures on the grounds that they run counter to personal freedoms enshrined in the constitution and repeating the claims of more con-servative advocates that the lockdowns are political motivated.

Some of those Americans who protest restrictions and who back Trump's claims that the election result is invalid cite conspiracy theories. Restrictions were framed as the first step towards authori-tarian government under which Americans will be subjected to lim-itations on their ownership of guns, further freedoms of movement and a complete erosion of what is termed the American way of life. As discussed in Chapter 3, while assessing a new message, citizens often depend on mental shortcuts and heuristics. Conspiracy the-ories provide the most powerful heuristics. They easily manipulate those who hold strong beliefs and prejudices and create feelings of anger and anxiety. The four factors discussed in Chapter 4 and indi-cated as necessary to induce a political action (acceptability, avail-ability, deemed urgency and the social eye) are thus formed. Some citizens rejected the health risks and took to the streets to demand their freedoms.

The contrasting levels of coherence across nations and the communication strategies of leaders are not the only way to explain the stark differences. Many of the nations who imposed lockdown also introduced an economic package to support businesses and employees laid off during lockdown. No new measures were introduced in the US, those made unemployed could apply for government aid but the impact of ten million claimants overloaded the system quickly. The blanket $1,200 for each American taxpayer had little real impact for the hardest hit. Facing a period with no income but normal household bills remaining the same and costs of normal consumer items simultaneously rising due to higher demands, it is little surprise that some protested. Such lived privations will also have led many to have sympathy with the tragic case of George Floyd, whose death was the result of his frustration at being accused of having a fake $20 bill so preventing him buying cigarettes. The privations felt by many Americans, coupled with claims that Covid-19 is a politically motivated hoax, shifted emotional responses from fear to anger and were expressed within the protests which included a heavily armed militia occupying the Michigan statehouse to demand an end to all restrictions.

Thursday April 30 2020 witnessed many events under the umbrella of the 'American Patriots Rally' calling for a return to work. The Michigan legislature, controlled by the Republican Party and despite 3,788 people having lost their lives to the virus within the state and having over 41,000 confirmed cases, refused the request of Democrat Governor Gretchen Whitmer to extend emergency measures. This opened up possibilities that Michigan businesses and citizens could sue the governor while her executive powers meant she had the power to extend the measures regardless of the decision in the legislature. Michigan thus witnessed a battle between different partisan ideologies, ones which remained polarised in the November election, and competing wings of government, both of which are democratically elected. The opinion of the mass of Michigan citizens is unknown, although a poll on April 19 2020 by Democrat-supporting media outlets NBC and The Washington Post showed that 58% of Americans were more concerned about relaxing the lockdown while 32% were more concerned about the economic impact. However, it seems a small number of protestors, given succour by President Trump and suggesting lockdowns need to be lifted, and conservative advocacy groups and their supportive media, have support of the Michigan legislative. Meanwhile, Michigan governor Whitmer pursued an alternative course underpinned by a different set of values. The division in the polls may reflect stark societal differences. 11.8% of US citizens were said to be living in poverty according to the 2018 census. It is likely this number has grown. Citizens often make their choices based on their political values. As explained in Chapters 2 and 4, materialists value basic resources required for their survival such as jobs and economic resources. It is highly possible that the have-nots mainly constitute the group opposing lockdown. With a minimal safety net, they are the most vulnerable to unemployment, increased poverty and becoming homeless and so may seek succour in arguments that suggest lockdown can be lifted. In contrast, a less financially insecure majority may be able to trust the validity of the restrictions as their livelihoods are not as seriously impacted and can view the crisis through a more post-materialist lens. The pandemic, and the 2020 election result, may expose deep divisions in the US between haves and have-nots, materialists and post-materialists, rather than a simple pro-Biden versus a pro-Trump camp.

Crises like the pandemic are naturally times of heightened anxiety. Anxiety "leads to a bias towards threatening news" (Albertson & Gadarian, 2015). Politicians, media and experts in democracies have more responsibility ever to cooperate and craft clear, consistent messages that aim to create solidarity and convince citizens to act responsibly. As explained in Chapter 1, citizens need to feel they belong to the society, that they are empowered and represented during the pandemic; leaders must build a culture of we-ness by embodying 'representing us', 'doing it for us' and crafting and embedding a sense of us in all communication (Jetten et al., 2002, pp. 25–30). Furthermore, to regulate distress, leaders are required to be transparent in their decision-making. Ardern's government appears to have accomplished this through the government alert level framework which assisted citizens in making sense of what was happening and why (Wilson, 2020). Where leaders play down risks, focus on divisions within society as opposed to calling for unity and offer no instruments to alleviate privations, anxiety turns to anger which fuels a desire to find an explanation. Some can find an answer in the conspiracy theories that in the US have linked Democrat state administrations with pro-China conspiracies and a hidden plan to restrict the freedoms Americans see as core to their constitution. Research shows that holding conspiracy beliefs is both a result of lack of trust in institutions as well as a cause of deepening mistrust in democratic processes. It is this mental state that leads to lower levels of adherence to containment-related guidance and legislation (Imhoff & Lamberty, 2020). Preventing the rise of conspiracy theories is a key duty of social media organisations and governments, despite the impinging of free speech. The recent invasion of the Capitol, the seat of the American democracy, has clearly displayed the dangers posed when conspiracy theories become prevalent among sections of society. Adherents of the QAnon movement, an extreme movement based on conspiracy theories, were on the front lines of the Capitol riot. The riot displayed to the world the danger that conspiracy theories can create (Argentino, 2021).

## DEMOCRACY WITHOUT ANXIETY

Understanding the psychology of democracy allows us to identify a variety of challenges that democratic institutions currently face. They appear not to meet expectations in terms of representing the people effectively. Citizens appear to be turning their back on democracy, some are mobilised by nongovernmental issue-oriented pressure groups, others by populists whose rhetoric deepens the divisions between citizens and their democratically elected representatives. While democracy should be agonistic, as per Mouffe (1999), it should not be antagonistic. Agonism involves respect for different positions; antagonism does not. Social disparities explain to some extent the parsing of political engagement, exposing the dangers that societal inequalities pose for cohesion and increased antagonism. If increasing numbers of citizens seek the security of echo chambers and have their prejudices reinforced or magnified, mistrust and dissatisfaction in democracy can only increase and spread. The glimmer of hope for democracies is perhaps found alongside the gloomier perspective we get from looking at the US. American politics is naturally an exceptional case. The constitutional arrangements, societal values and underpinning principles are in many ways unique. Equally, the style of leadership offered by Trump was sharpening divisions long prior to the pandemic hitting the nation. Australia, New Zealand, Canada, Scandinavian countries and even Ghana (Lilleker et al., 2021) offer better examples of how democratic institutions can be strengthened through offering a more reassuring, transparent, clear and inclusive style of leadership through a pandemic.

In their work *Together Apart*, which set out best practice rules for leaders bringing a nation together to collectively minimise the risks posed by Covid-19, Jetten et al. (2020) argued that citizens need to feel they belong, they are represented and they are listened to and understood. Leaders need to make them feel they are as safe and secure as is possible, and that the government and all democratic institutions are focused on serving the interests of all. Reminding readers of the core principles raised in the first chapters, in order to trust in democratic institutions, people need to feel empowered and significant, both as members of a society and through the processes of democracy, and trust that democracy will work equally well for everyone. In short, citizens need to trust that the democratic principles enshrined in legislation will actually be reflected in their everyday experiences of and interactions with the institutions of the state. Failure in any of these dimensions means citizens will lack trust in democratic institutions.

Therefore, within the persuasion and campaigning that modern politics necessitates, politicians must embody, through communication and action, representing all the people and working on behalf of all the people. Political leaders, candidates for office, or parties seeking government should not exacerbate divisions in society but heal them. The US proved a bad example. While equality is enshrined in the Constitution and Bill of Rights, what divides America is used, albeit in private, on the campaign trail. In 2012, Republican candidate Mitt Romney declared at a fundraiser that 47% of American voters were "dependent upon government . . . believe that they are victims . . . believe the government has a responsibility to care for them . . . believe that they are entitled to health care, to food, to housing".[1] These millions of Americans, Romney declared, would never vote Republican and would back Obama no matter what. Four years later, Democrat candidate Hillary Clinton, speaking at a similar event, described half of Donald Trump's supporters as a "basket of deplorables" who were "racist, sexist, homophobic, xenophobic, Islamophobic".[2] Such declarations signal that large swathes of Americans are unlikely to be represented by that candidate and that it may be unlikely they will work on behalf of the people they have written off as citizens that will not give them their vote. While these are statements designed for a private audience that were made public, they evidence that on the campaign trail, some citizens are seen as outside of the orbit of that candidate's target voter group. Once made public, they give the impression that the attitudes of these voters will also not be considered in the decision-making process. In an age of identity and issue politics, where affective polarisation can divide societies, when it is easier to retreat into an echo chamber than engage in open, pluralist debate, developing messages that will unify the public becomes more and more crucial for politicians.

In her acceptance speech Jacinda Ardern declared

> governing for every New Zealander has never been so important more than it has been now. We are living in an increasingly polarized world, a place where more and more people have lost the ability to see one another's point of view. I hope that this election, New Zealand has shown that this is not who we are. That as a nation, we can listen, and we can debate.[3]

The values espoused in this are not unique. However, they capture well the spirit of a way of performing politics that has the potential to increase trust and satisfaction, bring a nation together around a set of ideals and make people feel they belong to a functional democratic nation. Unlike his predecessor, Joe Biden adopted an inclusive rhetoric in his inauguration speech. Acknowledging the importance of shared values, Biden declared, "What are the common objects we as Americans love, that define us as Americans? I think we know. Opportunity, security, liberty, dignity, respect, honour, and yes, the truth" (Penna, 2021). Biden thus reminded the divided American nation of their shared identity. Citizens are often not preoccupied with their large group identities in their daily life but are more focused on their subgroup (Volkan, 2004). Reminding them of their national identity, and the core values of the nation, is important as national identity is so closely tied to the core identity of citizens, their sense of who they are and their sense of sameness with others in their nation. It can thus connect the public, create belonging and encourage unity and trust that the leader shares those values.

Biden's speech also made reference to the collective memories of American public:

> Through civil war, the Great Depression, World War, 9/11, through struggle, sacrifice, and setback, our better angels have always prevailed. In each of our moments enough of us have come together to carry all of us forward and we can do that now. History, faith and reason show the way. The way of unity. . . . If we do that, I guarantee we will not fail. We have never, ever, ever, ever failed in America when we've acted together.
>
> (Penna, 2021)

Here, Biden makes sure collective memories remain vivid in the nation's mind. This is important, as collective memories serve to maintain unity and increase the willingness of citizens to cooperate with other group members (Gongaware, 2003). Biden also included in his speech a reassurance to Trump's supporters that he will fight for them: "I will be a President for all Americans, all Americans. And I promise you I will fight for those who did not support me as for those who did" (Penna, 2021). Adopting an inclusive rhetoric, Biden thus drew a picture of an American president who will represent and fight for the whole nation. For a more vibrant democracy, more effort should be paid to building an inclusive single identity and societal and political trust. Particularly in the face of turbulent times, such as those caused by the pandemic, communication is crucial for reducing tensions and relieving anxiety. Recent events in the US have showed that politicians can foster inclusivity, a prerequisite for pluralist democracy, by welcoming differences in the society and bringing citizens together. Determining shared goals and objectives is also important but more important than this is working to meet these objectives. The popularity of Ardern in New Zealand proves to the world that attitudes and action can communicate more than words when they are executed wisely. While pluralism creates agonism, it also fosters respect and dialogue. An antagonistic society is one riven by inequality and division; neither of these provide the security that is required for citizens to have positive feelings towards democratic institutions.

## NOTES

1 www.politifact.com/factchecks/2012/sep/18/mitt-romney/mitt-romney-says-voters-who-support-barack-obama-a/
2 www.bbc.co.uk/news/av/election-us-2016-37329812
3 www.rev.com/blog/transcripts/new-zealand-pm-jacinda-ardern-victory-speech-transcript-wins-2020-new-zealand-election

## REFERENCES

Albertson, B., & Gadarian, S. K. (2015). *Anxious politics: Democratic citizenship in a threatening world.* Cambridge University Press.

Argentino, M. A. (2021, January 7). QAnon and the storm of the U.S. Capitol: The offline effect of online conspiracy theories. *The Conversation.* https://bit.ly/3c444Mj

Boland, B. (2020). How has New Zealand been so successful in managing covid-19?. *The BMJ*. https://blogs.bmj.com/bmj/2020/11/06/billy-boland-how-have-new-zealand-been-so-successful-in-managing-covid-19/

Gongaware, T. B. (2003). Collective memories and collective identities. *Journal of Contemporary Ethnography*, 32(5), 483–520. https://doi.org/10.1177/0891241603255674

Graham-McLay, C. (2020, September 23). Jacinda Ardern's Covid success gives national little room to move on policy. *The Guardian*. www.theguardian.com/world/2020/sep/23/jacinda-arderns-covid-success-gives-national-little-room-to-move-on-policy

Imhoff, R., & Lamberty P. (2020). A bioweapon or a hoax? The link between distinct conspiracy beliefs about the coronavirus disease (Covid-19) outbreak and pandemic behaviour. *Social Psychological and Personality Science*, 11(18), 1110–1118. https://doi.org/10.1177/1948550620934692

Jetten, J., Postmes, T., & McAuliffe, B. (2002). We're all individuals: Group norms of individualism and collectivism, levels of identification and identity threat. *European Journal of Social Psychology*, 32(2), 189–207. https://doi.org/10.1002/ejsp.65

Jetten, J., Reicher, S. D., Haslam, S. A., & Cruwys, T. (Eds.). (2020). Together Apart: The Psychology of COVID-19. Sage.

Lilleker, D., Coman, I., Gregor, M., & Novelli, E. (2021). Political communication and COVID-19: Governance and rhetoric in global comparative perspective. In D. Lilleker, I. Coman, M. Gregor, & E. Novelli (Eds.), *Political communication and covid-19: Governance and rhetoric in times of crisis* (pp. 333–350). Routledge. https://doi.org/10.4324/9781003120254

Mouffe, C. (1999). Deliberative democracy or agonistic pluralism? *Social Research*, 66(3), 745–758. www.jstor.org/stable/pdf/40971349.pdf

Penna, D. (2021, April 21). President Joe Biden's inauguration speech in full: "We will write an American story of hope". *The Telegraph*. https://bit.ly/3bXvX8H

Volkan, V. (2004). *Blind trust: Large groups and their leaders in times of crisis and terror*. Pitchstone Publishing.

Wilson, S. (2020, April 5). Three reasons why Jacinda Ardern's coronavirus response has been a masterclass in crisis leadership. *The Conversation*. https://bit.ly/3p9MSca

## FURTHER READING

Albertson, B., & Gadarian, S. K. (2015). *Anxious politics: Democratic citizenship in a threatening world*. Cambridge University Press.

Lilleker, D., Coman, I., Gregor, M., & Novelli, E. (2021). Political communication and COVID-19: Governance and rhetoric in global comparative perspective. In D. Lilleker, I. Coman, M. Gregor, & E. Novelli (Eds.), *Political communication and covid-19: Governance and rhetoric in times of crisis* (pp. 333–350). Routledge.

Printed in the United States
by Baker & Taylor Publisher Services